"Mike Felix's book, **The Diversity Dilemma**, rightfully calls out corporate America for their decades long failure to achieve meaningful diversity. They focused on race instead of what Felix says is the most important factor: development. We have a chance to get true diversity in today's America that goes beyond skin color and Felix's book provides us with the invaluable guidelines."

—**Corey Brooks, Senior Pastor at New Beginnings Church of Chicago, Social Change Agent, Board President ProjectHOOD, Entrepreneur**

"Every culture war needs a peacemaker with a plan to resolve it. *The Diversity Dilemma* is an actionable guide that can transform relationships, culture, companies— and most importantly, yourself. Mike Felix doesn't just talk about these principles; he lives them, and what he has written is tried, tested, and fruitful. If you possess even a small measure of self-reflective courage, applying these groundbreaking truths will lead to an immeasurable impact. Read it with an open heart, and countless hearts and lives will be touched and changed."

—*Karl Clauson, Pastor, Radio Host, author of* **Thrill, The 7 Resolutions,** *and* **Killing Sin**

"**The Diversity Dilemma** is a transformative guide to leadership that not only confronts the failures of traditional diversity initiatives but offers a powerful, actionable model for meaningful change. Mike Felix masterfully connects leadership development with organizational performance, illustrating how intentional mentoring can unlock the potential of underrepresented talent. As a brilliant leader and true Multiplier, Mike equips you to elevate others, expand your bench strength, and build a high-performing, future-ready organization."

—*Liz Wiseman, Bestselling author of* **Multipliers, Rookie Smarts,** *and* **Impact Players**

Mike Felix, Ph.D.

THE DIVERSITY DILEMMA

Equipping Your Organization to
Turn Potential into Performance

Story BUILDERS PRESS

Published by StoryBuilders Press
Paperback: 978-1-954521-86-5
eBook: 978-1-954521-85-8

CONTENTS

AUTHOR'S NOTE

The great sociologist of the 1970s, Marshall McLuhan, gave us this maxim: *The Medium Is the Message.* What lies on the pages of this book are the facts, justifications, and stories of people whose careers were impacted by personal investment.

Just like investments in the market, not every investment has the same payoff. But certainly, not to invest is to ensure that there will be no gains at all.

What does this have to do with Marshall McLuhan? In today's fast-paced business environment of change and achievement, it's easy to get caught up in all the technologies afforded to us for personal assessment and development. What gets missed are the opportunities for personal investments in people—especially those who would otherwise get little to no investment from more senior and more effective leaders. That personal investment *is* the medium that matters most. It says, "You are important" and "You are worthy" of the time to *help you be the best version of yourself.*

My intention is to make you think about how to ensure both equal development of your people and long-term sustainability of diversity in your organization. While some organizations are better than others, the evidence suggests that there is still quite a way to go in corporate America.

INTRODUCTION

A sign of a good leader is not how many followers you have, but how many leaders you create.
—*Mahatma Gandhi*

This book is based on two indisputable truths. First, employees who have the attention and investment of someone far more senior in the organization will rise more quickly and, ultimately, higher in the organization. Second, sustainable diversity in the more senior ranks of any organization is less about equal opportunity and far more about the development opportunities people receive.

Development is best facilitated through mentoring relationships because these relationships foster feedback—the wonderful gift that helps us see ourselves as others see us. There have been many books on the subject of mentoring in the last ten to fifteen years, each with a particular point of view on how to do mentoring effectively. None of them, however, addresses this pressing issue: How does effective mentoring relate to achieving and sustaining diversity at all levels of the organization?

Diversity initiatives and Equal Employment Opportunity compliance are well-intentioned and certainly great for the annual report, but after four decades, these efforts still haven't produced the kind of diversity that is representative of the culture, especially in the C-suite and among senior executive ranks of corporate America.

Why is that?

Diversity, as viewed by many corporations, is often conceptualized as an opportunity-driven effort to allow diverse candidates to apply for or be considered for any particular position. Some organizations view diversity as meeting prescribed targets for the mix of employees from underrepresented groups. Others see it as ensuring that no particular group dominates the majority of all the positions on a team or in a department.

The preparation for such opportunities is completely on the shoulders of each prospective candidate. The tacit belief is that leaders are born. But I disagree with this notion. Researchers such as Isabel Briggs Myers and Katharine Cook Briggs, as well as Jack Zenger and Joe Folkman, will tell you that the world of top leaders is almost evenly split between extroverts and introverts. We see born extroverts with an imposing presence as leaders. How, then, can born introverts command a presence? This is a learned trait—generally taught by someone such as a parent, teacher, coach, or mentor—and developed over time.

As I found out when interviewing and considering diverse candidates for leadership positions, a higher-than-average percentage of them lacked awareness of the necessary leadership skills, behaviors, and competencies required for success in the job. To put it simply, they were not prepared to move to the next level of responsibility.

Everyone knew the potential position would present opportunities for growth, but most were unaware of what needed to change in themselves or the areas for growth and development required to succeed in the job. The next level up for them was a big step with more than just incremental demands. The job required a different set of leadership skills and competencies for them to be successful.

What I found in each candidate was a view that the necessary preparation for the job consisted of a checklist of experiences, education, and certifications. Experience is important—more important in some jobs than in others—but it is not a primary predictor of success for any job. For that matter, neither is past performance. What experience and performance should have provided were opportunities to grow and change. We assume that because we have one (experience), we have the other (growth). This assumption is why leaders—diverse or not—flame out in a higher-level job or in their careers, often referred to as the Peter principle.[1]

As anyone who has overcome obstacles to arrive at positions of leadership will tell you, some of the best lessons on the qualities, competencies, and characteristics of highly effective leaders are learned through mentoring. That is, a personal investment made by a more senior person to improve their leadership effectiveness.

These leaders are what Jim Collins describes in his book *Good to Great* as level 5 leaders—the kind who drive extraordinary results in their organizations. My experience taught me that I needed to create an intentional, safe, and permanent space in my organization where this type of mentoring and diversity could successfully meet.

The two concepts of mentoring and diversity are seldom brought together programmatically and intentionally to develop a high-performance diverse leadership structure. If an effective mentoring program were in place that focused on equal development of people, hiring managers should be able to select candidates from a pool of diverse candidates for greater responsibilities and assignments, with recommendations from more senior executives who had mentored them.

My purpose in writing this book is to put these two concepts together in a program that you can use to build your organization around a stated commitment to growing diverse leaders and a diverse leadership bench—a roster of qualified candidates from which people may be confidently selected for increasing responsibility.

In chapter 6, you'll find the program that I built and continue to use to this day. It is a series of reading, writing, and application assignments, using material from thought leaders that continues to be relevant today. It is organized to lead the mentee on a process of discovery, change, building an enduring brand, and motivating and leading people to full engagement, achieving more than they thought possible. These are the kinds of leaders who are fully prepared for leadership at the next level and above.

The reader may find exceptions to almost anything I've written in this book, but the outlier story here or there does not disprove what I've said. The collection of data becomes the compelling evidence of the truth, and the data show that, overwhelmingly, diverse candidates find it more difficult to make their way up the organizational ladder.

While diversity may exist at the entry level in many companies, it diminishes with each level toward the top leadership ranks in most companies. Companies for which this is a problem may proudly exclaim that they support diversity, but this is tantamount to virtue signaling if there is no purposeful plan to establish development opportunities and promote leaders who put feet to the values of diversity.

Diversity isn't so much about equal *opportunity*, where diverse candidates may apply or even interview for jobs. It's about equal *development*: ensuring that everyone who desires advancement gets an equal opportunity to be developed into the kind of leader who will produce results and excel both inside and outside the organization. This process of equal development is intentional, structured, and programmed. It is here that relationships and commitment help personal stories, aspirations, and careers change trajectories.

1 ENLIGHTENMENT

*Learn to listen. Opportunity could be knocking
at your door very softly.*
—*Frank Tyger*

I was a senior executive for a Fortune 50 company that had a stated commitment to diversity and inclusion. Some segments of the company were diverse by most standards, but many segments fell short of any meaningful diversity standard—especially at more senior ranks. Short of becoming egalitarian by mandating diversity goals, this lack of diversity translated to more homogeneous leadership with each successive level rising through the organization.

In one of the divisions I led, a senior executive had elected to move to a different assignment within the company, and so I began looking for candidates to fill this key role. At the time, I was just trying to fill the position and not necessarily thinking about how to change the trajectory on diversity. The selected candidate just had to be able to succeed in the job and help raise the overall performance level of the organization. Putting anyone in the job—diverse or not—only to watch them "flame out" or fail was not the right decision for either the potential candidate or the organization.

I knew from my research on hiring practices that there was so much more to consider than just experience, education, achievement, or competencies. None of these were good predictors of success in the role (or in any role).

Having been asked to lead this organization because it was perennially in last place among the other major divisions, I felt the pressure to install a leader who could lead this sizable group to a higher level of performance. I didn't have the time to experiment with different leaders to see if they would "sink or swim." My success in the turnaround effort was dependent on finding the right people for key jobs—the first time. This meant finding a leader who had already exhibited the right leadership behaviors to build trust and engagement and inspire employees to a higher level of performance.

My human resources partner, who was in an underrepresented employee group herself, worked diligently to find diverse internal candidates who were qualified for the position.

After a couple of months of searching, she came to me and said, "Mike, there aren't any qualified, diverse candidates to put into the pipeline for consideration for promotion."

We had several diverse candidates in first-line manager positions, but stepping into the vacant role would have been a double promotion for these candidates. The lack of time and development that comes with a single-step promotion into a second-level role would almost guarantee failure. That was a bet I wasn't willing to make—especially in a turnaround effort.

WE HAVE A PROBLEM

For my part, I began to ponder the question of why. Why couldn't we find qualified, diverse candidates for consideration of stepping into the role? Qualified candidates from outside my organization applied for the job, but none of them wanted to relocate from their warm-weather cities. Doing the job and leading people from a remote location was not going to work. I had been doing turnarounds successfully for twenty years prior, and I knew firsthand that being remote while attempting to lead more than 1,500 people was not a recipe for success.

For my employees' part, many of them were wondering if my stated commitment to diversity was going to have any bearing on whom I selected for the vacant role. Some were emboldened to apply, believing they could succeed in the role. However, filling the position with a candidate solely because they were diverse wasn't going to work if they didn't have the capacities, competencies, and behaviors to succeed. That would not have been fair to them, and it certainly wasn't going to advance the culture ultimately toward a more diverse leadership team.

MEETING JANET

After interviewing all the candidates who had applied to be considered for the leadership position, one of them—a female in an underrepresented group, Janet—called me. Even though I had allowed her to interview for the position, I was struggling with how to tell her that she wasn't really qualified.

To my surprise, however, she already knew that but wanted to interview anyway because she wanted to find out what it took to do the job. In her words, "I don't think I'll ever get a chance for a promotion unless I have some visibility."

A fair point.

What flashed through my mind was this question: How do I give diverse candidates better visibility—not just for my organization, but also for opportunities in the larger company? For Janet's part, she asked a compelling question (my paraphrase): "If I need visibility to get ahead, but can't get visibility because I don't qualify, how do I break this doom cycle and get an opportunity?"

I'm quite sure Janet must have been wondering if I had any idea what she was trying to convey, and yet she desperately wanted to know if my actions would match my words about valuing a diverse organization.

While people may not openly verbalize this question, every underrepresented employee in your organization is asking it, desperately wanting someone in leadership to answer it with actions. I felt like this conversation deserved more than just a "thanks, but no thanks" conclusion to the selection process.

As we talked, I explained that even visibility won't help if you don't have the ability to succeed. To her credit, she wanted more feedback on just what she needed to have to be seriously considered. Like every other candidate I had interviewed for the job, Janet wanted to point to her achievements, experience, education, and past performance reviews as the justifications for being ready for the role.

I knew that none of these were adequate predictors of success in the role, and after a few open-ended questions about examples of key behaviors from previous jobs and leadership positions, she got the point.

This begged the question: How do I teach younger and aspiring executives to have the right leadership behaviors so they can build a track record and gain visibility by the way they lead?

It was in the middle of this conversation, while trying to lean in and show some empathy and compassion—and with all these questions swirling around in my head—that my aha moment hit me like a bolt of lightning.

Immediately, I realized that if I really valued diversity, I had to be committed to building a strong and diverse leadership team. I had to have a role in *preparing* people—and especially diverse and underrepresented people—for higher performance and greater responsibility.

I owed it to all the diverse candidates in my organization to provide more than just words and opportunities to interview. Sure, they would feel good about the opportunity, but if none were selected because they hadn't demonstrated great leadership behaviors, what message would I be sending to the organization and the candidates who interviewed?

My commitment to diversity had to be seen in my actions.

Investing in people to build a diverse bench of qualified potential candidates for any elevated role would be chief among them. Just as importantly, I had to provide underrepresented employees with an equal opportunity for this type of development. This was the only way to ensure that when future opportunities for advancement came along, we would indeed have a pool of qualified and diverse candidates.

THE PROBLEM WITH SELF-REPORTING

Before we ended the call, I admitted to Janet that I had gotten it all wrong. I could no longer hold to the notion that she and her colleagues across my organization should just keep on applying and interviewing until "they figure it out." It was my job as a leader to ensure that she and her colleagues could interview with confidence for a job at the next level, knowing they had the leadership chops to succeed.

Unfortunately, until her interview with me, Janet hadn't realized she was not qualified. She honestly felt like her accomplishments had at least earned her an interview. Her performance reviews were average. She had completed her bachelor's degree while she was employed by the company. She had even attended a couple of leadership classes and received a few certificates for training and self-development.

But none of that helped me answer the right question in hiring her: *Did she display the leadership behaviors to succeed in this elevated position with ten times the responsibility?*

While we talked, her comments regarding her preparedness for the job made me realize my own shortcomings in getting to know the development needs of the emerging leaders who worked in my organization. I had fallen into the trap that snares so many companies, where leadership development is a one-size-fits-all (some better than others) approach to leadership development.

My tacit expectation was that people would self-select into the areas where they felt they needed development, and the ones who were successful in figuring it out would be the ones who were ready for bigger opportunities. But I knew from my psychology training that isn't how it works.

In the 1970s, Professors Richard Nisbett and Timothy DeCamp Wilson at the University of Michigan found that apart from outside stimuli—feedback—"we do not have [mental] access to the cognitive processes that help us understand what we do and why we do it."[2] This research has been corroborated several times, especially in the work of Sheila Heen and Doug Stone in their book, *Thanks for the Feedback*, and by Daniel Kahneman and Amos Tversky as outlined in Kahneman's book *Thinking Fast and Slow*.

In other words, we are poor at self-reporting. That is, we don't see ourselves as accurately as others see us.

The only thing that changes our ability to see ourselves accurately is this wonderful gift called feedback. In an organization where feedback comes once a year (which is one of the reasons I'm not a fan of the annual performance review), and is often disingenuous, how does one get enough feedback and coaching to make a lasting and substantial difference in one's career trajectory?

Since I was new to the organization, the signs of horrible annual performance reviews were all around me. Like it or not, these performance reviews leave people with the notion that "if I just change this one outcome, I'll get a better review next time and hopefully get a bigger raise."

For Janet's part, her performance reviews were average in that she had been rated "Meets

Expectations" to "Fully Meets Expectations" (I never really understood the nuanced difference), with a few "Exceeds Expectations" thrown in. These ratings, according to the directions sent out by HR, were to be reflective of two dimensions of performance: *"What* did I accomplish?" and *"How* did I accomplish it?"* Dysfunction abounds in organizations where meeting or exceeding the "what" gives one a license to marginalize or even ignore the "how."

Yet for many performance reviews, the end justifies the means.

How did I know this? Quite simple. Spending time with employees in any organization will reveal this phenomenon. They are uninspired. They do just enough to meet expectations. They don't trust leaders, and there is no sense of team. While I was new to this assignment, I had been doing turnarounds even before I arrived at my current company. In fact, the company had originally hired me to turn around a remote and stand-alone business unit.

Success in turnarounds comes from making quick assessments as to where the dysfunction is, which processes and lines of communication are broken, and assessing who should stay and who should go. In a turnaround situation, one typically has only weeks to a few months to figure this out. The leaders in an organization can rarely admit where the dysfunction lies or what's broken. In their minds, the problems are always elsewhere.

If you want to know what's broken and where the dysfunction originates, you have to do a lot of MBWA (management by walking around). I always made it a point to stay out of my office and spend time talking to the people who do all the real work in an organization: those who work with customers or turn out a product. This habit stood me in good stead in this new assignment. Even though I had been in position for just a few months, I had been to places and talked to people who hadn't seen anyone at my level in the previous twenty-five or so years. I had spent enough time with the frontline workers and the first line of management to know exactly what kind of performance reviews people were getting and that making the numbers at almost all costs was rampant across the organization, justifying bad leadership behaviors and creating a culture of self-protection. Ironically, for all the emphasis on making the numbers (the "what"), the division had never been out of last place, which was why I was asked to go there.

The leaders in this division had been exposed to the same training and development opportunities as every other leader across the company. But self-select development clearly wasn't working. Annual performance reviews were not getting the intended results in leadership behavior changes. The culture was in the ditch.

The only way to turn this around was to start investing in people.

And it was in this context that Janet was brave enough to tell me that *no one had ever taken the time to show her how to be a better leader.* She wanted more opportunities and a chance at advancement, but short of accumulating more training certificates and higher education, she didn't know how to get there.

By the end of the conversation, she was almost in tears, and I was feeling like I had let her down, along with all her colleagues across the organization. It was time to stop *admiring the problem* and begin to step in and start *doing* something to solve it.

THE PROBLEM WITH ADMIRING THE PROBLEM

Although this Fortune 50 company supplied its leaders with many opportunities to learn, from annual in-person workshops and strategy sessions, to online courses or modules, to monographs and books, I could see that this hadn't worked out so well in uniformly developing leaders.

In any of these settings, people would have limited engagement with the material and would typically only select something they were interested in, but as we've already discussed, likely not what they needed most. Senior executives like me would attend an annual leadership summit with our colleagues from across the company. There we would hear from thought leaders and authors handpicked to deliver thought-provoking presentations on a variety of topics from strategy and markets to human development, personal improvement, and leadership. We would also engage in group exercises to reinforce the themes of the summit.

Occasionally, we got a TEDx version of a senior executive's story, but as inspirational as some of them were, they didn't show us what we should do or how we could be better leaders. While these talks raised our collective awareness of others and the obstacles that some had to overcome, only a portion of the audience could identify with the background or circumstances of the speaker.

But after a few years, I began to realize that these learning opportunities had only marginally, or at best, incrementally impacted the way we went about our leadership development. During some of these events, senior leaders from inside the company would participate in on-stage panel discussions regarding many of these topics: how we need to do this or that and the relative benefits we could reap if we did. No one ever made it personal. No one ever stood up and said, "This is what I was doing that held us back. Here's how I found out, this is what I changed, and this is what happened."

I have a name for this. I call this *admiring the problem*.

Bringing a learning format such as this to my organization was not going to accomplish what I needed in terms of building a diverse bench. I couldn't guarantee that everyone would engage, and I couldn't guarantee there would be the kind of behavior changes needed for meaningful performance improvement across the management ranks.

My "enlightening" phone conversation with Janet and the exhaustive search for qualified diverse candidates to fill a key leadership position challenged my thinking and forced me to reevaluate my own view of diversity and how to achieve it while getting to higher levels of performance. I was just as guilty of admiring the problem. In the context of that aha moment with Janet, I realized that any commitment to diversity had to be more than just raising awareness and creating momentary inspiration for people. It had to be about developing and growing a diverse bench of qualified candidates to succeed at not just the next level but two to three successive levels upward.

This begged two questions for me:

1. *What was my active role going to be to ensure equal investment in people?*
2. *How was I going to engage the mentees in such a way as to create a commitment to lasting change and development?*

As I pondered these two questions, I knew that how I answered them would determine whether we would create the kind of performance improvement we needed for the turnaround and, at the same time, build a diverse and qualified bench of available candidates ready for increased responsibility.

FROM IDEA TO EXECUTION

After I hung up the phone, the first question I asked myself was, *How am I going to do this?*

I had no idea what I had gotten myself into. My mind began to race with ideas on how to start to develop people, but I didn't really have a structure for the material I had gathered and used over the previous twenty years. Most of what I had was used in single sessions or a limited series of two to four sessions when I had to answer a burning question for a small group looking for advice and counsel.

Even though I didn't have all the details ironed out, early on in my thought processes, I knew that creating a learning and development track for mentees would be foundational to helping them be the best version of themselves that they could be. The best way to bring about the kind of performance improvements we needed was to change people's career trajectories. Further, If I invested in the right people, I figured I could also change the diversity profile of my management organization.

One of the reasons that the Girls Who Code movement gained so much momentum was the recognition that if we're going to change the males-to-females ratio in the computer sciences, we must provide opportunities for young women to have an equal development track to the one that young men are predominantly exposed to—and as early. Introducing the entire population of young people to the same development at the same age is the surest way to change the diversity mix.

Recently, in recognition of the same phenomenon, the United States Golf Association announced the creation of a "development league." This was the USGA's version of a mentoring program designed to provide underrepresented groups the very same development opportunities as those who are raised in a country club environment.

Within corporate America, opportunities for such development are typically organized and controlled by corporate training departments. However, the best way to ensure that a leadership team is diverse, all the way to the C-suite—just like in the Girls Who Code initiative—is to provide equal opportunity for development through mentoring with the goal of developing the person and the leader within.

As one of the leading researchers in mentoring and its benefits, Lillian Eby et al. (2007) found that the personal investment that comes with mentoring is the surest way to prepare others with the skills, competencies, attitudes, and behaviors to succeed and to change one's career trajectory.

Further, because employees are individuals, all of whom have a basic need to "belong," mentoring also instills, promotes, and perpetuates an organization's culture so that values, traditions, rituals, and unspoken rules of navigating the organization are passed onto the next generation of leaders.[3] As the old management axiom goes, "Culture trumps strategy."

Without the kind of road map that comes with personal investment from someone higher in the organization, it's easy for leaders to tap out on their effectiveness and eventually erode the leadership capital they need to keep rising in an organization. Getting mentees to build trusting relationships with mentors and colleagues across all demographics—without regard to race, gender, culture, age, or beliefs—is the surest way to build and sustain a diverse bench of capable leaders. More than just creating opportunity windows for employees, getting them to enroll and commit to a process and journey of development is foundational to putting employees on a personal and career development trajectory that will outlive even a yearlong mentoring program.

Establishing a small group where trust, feedback, and accountability grow would also ensure that each mentee who desired to keep growing would have a support group to help keep them on a growth path. I wanted to make sure that everyone had the same foundation and prospects for success—even though, ultimately, people had to fail or succeed based on their own choices, behaviors, and leadership skills. It's just so much easier when one has the support of colleagues and the investment of a more senior leader.

In my mind, this was the point of productive mentoring relationships.

A PROGRAM IS BORN

About a week after my conversation with Janet, even though she didn't make it to the final round of interviews but was brave enough to challenge me, I called her back. I needed to create a different ending to her search for promotion and to tell her how much her comments made me realize that I had an active responsibility to not just support diversity but to build it and ensure its sustainability in the organization.

Having had a week to ponder the connections between and among feedback, development, investment, and diversity, I felt like I couldn't leave her feeling defeated about her interview experience. This was not going to help her feel like engaging as a productive member of the leadership team.

After describing to her the impact she had on my thinking, I asked her if she would allow me to invest in her to help her grow and to prepare her to not only *interview* successfully but to *succeed* at the next level. I owed her at least that much.

Her answer to my question was an emphatic "Yes!" I thanked her for being honest with me and told her that her boldness would forever change the way I viewed getting to and sustaining a diverse organization. But then her next question to me changed my paradigm. She asked if something like this could be available to her colleagues across our division who desired the same opportunity but didn't know how to approach me for it.

I answered her question with a question: "Would you be willing to find eleven of your colleagues across the division whom you believe deserve an opportunity for development?"

I told her that there was only one stipulation for this first group: no white males. And no, this was not a play for identity politics. I felt like I needed to show by my actions that I was committed to building diversity in my organization. So I enrolled her in helping me by finding eleven other diverse candidates across my organization that she felt were deserving of an opportunity to be similarly mentored. She needed to evaluate and discern who would be serious in their commitment to a yearlong program of learning and growing. This would be an opportunity for her to exercise discernment and an opportunity to keep any of my unconscious biases out of the decision on who should be mentored.

This small-group type of environment best facilitates people becoming vulnerable with each other, getting an accurate view of themselves and their development needs, mapping a path to personal and professional growth, and committing to a life and career of managing change—in themselves and their organizations. Any more than twelve people tends to diminish people's engagement with the material and with each other. In a small group, there is an element of safety, and yet, no place to hide.

We agreed that we would start the following month and that in addition to her role of selecting the other mentees, she was tasked with asking them to write an email to me stating that they were committed to the mentoring process for an entire year. One could argue—and my dearest friend reminds me—that the material really is a two-to-three-year process. However, in the corporate world where organizations can change in any given year, I felt like I had one year to make the biggest investment I could make and give my mentees the tools and material to sustain their leadership growth after our time together.

Eventually, I ended up mentoring everyone at her level, all the emerging leaders in the organization who expressed a desire to be mentored—no matter where they were in their careers. I was keenly aware that some would see this effort as a program for me to develop a bunch of "mini mes."

I certainly didn't need more of *me* in the organization. What I needed were leaders who could be their authentic selves and be effective at building, managing, and leading teams to higher performance. I also needed a diverse set of leaders who were confident enough to contribute their perspectives on how to solve some of the thorny operational problems we encountered that held us back from improving the performance of the division.

The following chapters contain the results of the research showing that the problem of building diversity at more senior ranks exists broadly across American businesses. As a result of my own change in thinking about how to build and sustain diversity,

I have included the learning and development track I used to help emerging leaders be the best version of themselves. While the program was refined in subsequent mentoring groups, it is still pretty close to its original incarnation. Lastly, I have included a chapter of comments directly from those who came through the mentoring program. Most, if not all, will tell you that the program was transformational for them.

And for the organization?

We took the division from dead last place by any measure—financial, performance, and safety—to first place in less than three years, all while building a diverse leadership structure.

2 WHY HAVE DIVERSITY INITIATIVES FAILED?

> *[Diversity] requires a deliberate, culturally*
> *intelligent process.*
> **—David Livermore**

Proponents of diversity say the empirical evidence shows that diverse organizations solve problems and innovate faster and more effectively and tend to rise to the top of their respective industry segments.

David Livermore, in his book *Driven by Difference* (2016), contends that diversity doesn't only ensure better innovation, but it also takes an intelligent connection to and understanding of the culture that the organization serves.[4] I would concur with his assessment and add that diversity alone doesn't ensure better performance. But diversity with investments in competencies and cultural sensitivities makes for better performance.

Because diverse thinking and perspectives, coupled with leadership competencies, help companies read the room better, these companies perform better across the spectrum of operational and administrative functions, from accounting and finance to sales and marketing, from research to operations, and every function in between.

While social job and career sites such as LinkedIn have seminars and learning modules to help users understand how to increase business performance and effectiveness by increasing diversity and cultural awareness, they stop short of offering the step of infusing great leadership competencies into a diverse organization.

One thing remains missing: None of these career sites addresses the question of how to reach and sustain diversity while maintaining a high level of performance. W. Edward Demming taught us all that if you want different outcomes in quality, you must fix the "inputs"—the actions and activities that increase quality and therefore quality outcomes.

So it is with diversity. Reaching diversity in an organization that requires high performance isn't accomplished by fixing the outcomes; it's done by fixing the inputs—getting a more diverse funnel of employees who are being invested in and building more effective leadership competencies.

As a result of diversity training and awareness— generally a required learning module in many corporations that embrace diversity—the entry-level workforce in American business may have become more representative of society, but at some level— generally in the mid- to senior-management ranks— diversity begins to fade and the corporate ranks become more and more homogenous. A dangerous disconnect happens because senior-level decision-making, where strategy and budgets are set, tends to become less diverse and removed from lower levels of management where execution of the strategy takes place.

TWO PROBLEMS

The evidence suggests there is one of two problems at work in these organizations: either (1) a bias toward choosing and investing in people who are familiar to leadership or (2) candidates for promotion aren't all equipped with the leadership, communication, or organizational skills and competencies needed to succeed at these higher levels. These problems are highlighted by a 2018 study from Pew Research, which found that women and people of color still have concerns of disparity and discrimination in STEM (science, technology, engineering, and math) jobs.[5]

Neither problem bodes well for building and sustaining diversity.

Claims of diversity at entry-level jobs and junior-level management positions are pointless if the diverse employees are tapped out for growth or can't really succeed at the next levels in the organization. This is an indication of how well diverse employees have been developed to succeed in these senior-level positions in companies. The intention to hire diverse candidates is admirable, but the lack of attention to their success and the lack of investment in their development work against all the measurable benefits that come with having a diverse workforce.

Just measuring the ratios of diverse or underrepresented people at various levels of the organization will not ensure that real diversity is taking place. It takes an *intentional plan of action* to change and sustain the diversity profile of any organization. This is tantamount to attempting to fix product quality issues by measuring defects. Any six-sigma quality expert will tell you that measuring defects without a resulting inspection of underlying processes is useless for changing outcomes.

It's more than just providing equal opportunity or equal access to be considered for higher positions; it's about ensuring that the bench of candidates has had equal opportunity for development.

DEI GOT IT WRONG

Forced outcomes, by promoting people who are not fully prepared with the skills, competencies, and behaviors needed for success in their new role—no matter what people group they represent—will result in decreased organizational performance that ultimately plays out in attrition, employee morale and engagement, operational performance, and ultimately, share price.

The Diversity, Equity, and Inclusion efforts of the past decade have not solved the diversity problem, but rather exacerbated a growing social tension on the issue of represented diversity. In a capitalistic society where shareholders expect returns for their investments in companies, performance and merit become the only valid measure of anyone's fitness for a given position affecting outcomes.

The DEI rubric, however, prioritized other factors ahead of these, with no real ability to predict neither success in the given role nor any future success. Categories and identity became the prioritized filter, but could not—and did not—account for behavioral predictors of one's performance. In fact, this has become such a failure for shareholders that several companies have begun to abandon their commitments to DEI and, with it, billions of dollars of lost shareholder value.

The not-so-subtle difference between a formal mentoring program represented in this book and a DEI (also known in some circles as EDI) initiative is found in the letter *E*. *E* stands for *equity*—which by its very definition, suggests that diversity and inclusion have taken place if the outcomes are equitable. In public companies, however, the only outcome that shareholders are concerned with is performance results.

What the movement failed to acknowledge was that if one wants performance and diversity to coexist, it can only happen when there is a diverse bench of equally qualified—right competencies and behaviors—candidates for any given position. And this can only happen when people have equally been given an opportunity for the kind of investment that builds leadership skills, competencies, and capacities needed to succeed and to grow. Equity requires a sponsor, or multiple sponsors, to keep score for the program. Equality in mentoring requires a sponsor to invest in people.

In a school district I'm familiar with, there is a principal no one likes to work with because of her attitude and overbearing style. She "checked" quite a few boxes with identity, education, and titles but was completely unaware of (or indifferent to) how people and their performance were affected by her leadership. Every time she moved to a new school in the system, teachers there started to transfer to other schools in the system. Some even left the school system for other opportunities.

With inadequate and ineffective leaders, employee churn goes up, and the organization is handicapped in its efforts to sustain its performance. This is a great example of promoting someone who checks all the right identity boxes, with all the right education and experiential qualifications for the position, but has not developed the behaviors, competencies, and social intelligence to be an effective leader.

THE REAL ENEMY OF DIVERSITY

Near the end of 2018, Google employees began rallying support for a shareholder proposal that called for the board of its parent company, Alphabet, to address issues related to gender and racial diversity and tying these metrics to executive compensation. The shareholder resolution also made clear that the lack of diversity in the tech sector is a "crisis that threatens worker safety, talent retention, product development, and customer service."[6]

Their resolution called out the glaring fact that diversity in Silicon Valley, in general, is a problem that has not been adequately addressed by boards and executive leadership across the tech industry. Google's employees had certainly received the tacit message from their leadership: Certain people groups are not valued for their diverse thinking and perspectives.

This message, intentional or not, reinforces a prevailing perception that the implicit view held by very senior levels across industry is that underrepresented groups are mostly not prepared to succeed much above their current positions. While measuring the mix of the employees at the various levels in the industry is important, no problem is ever fixed by just committing to measuring the outcomes better. Unless there is a programmatic and intentional way to prepare people for greater leadership roles, there will likely still be issues with achieving and sustaining diversity at more senior levels.

In June 2017, CEOs and senior executives from the United States' top 150 companies sent out a joint release about their companies' collective commitment to diversity in the workplace. The fact that there needed to be a formal announcement suggests recognition among these executives that the imbalances in women and minorities in many companies and especially among more senior ranks are very real and the mix of employees is not representative of the diversity in the culture. A close read of the release talks about diversity and inclusion as functions of opportunity.

When I started doing the research for this book, I discovered some telling facts. At the very senior executive ranks of the top 100 companies in the United States, as measured by *Fortune Magazine*, only 9 percent of the people were people of color (Black, Hispanic, Asian) and fewer than 22 percent were women. This was clearly not representative of the culture in which we live.

In the intervening years since I started the research, the era of "wokeness" has seen some things change. For example, people of color (Black, Hispanic, and Asian) now represent less than 19 percent of the senior executive ranks of the top 100 companies, and women occupy about 28 percent of the senior executive ranks. It's important to note that more than 85 percent of companies that instituted DEI policies for hiring and promotion have since abandoned those policies for reasons of cost or the inability to find the economic payoff or value creation for the policies.

Attempting to prescribe a target mix of employees and manage to an outcome makes the selection process nearly fait accompli. DEI policies aside, some companies provide equal opportunity to interview for open positions, leaving to chance the hiring decision and the candidate's ability to progress through the organization based on performance.

Neither of these approaches clearly solves the problem of how to ensure the long-term viability and sustainability of diversity across the organization.

Since the data indicates that the higher one rises in a company, the more homogenous the views, opinions, and perspectives become, without a purposeful effort to counter this, homogeneity becomes the enemy of diversity.

EQUAL OPPORTUNITY OR EQUAL DEVELOPMENT?

While opportunity is important—and certainly a necessary ingredient in diversity—to make better progress than we've made in the last forty years, diversity and inclusion must be about more than just equal opportunity; it must be about equal development. Without a plan for equal development, the push for equal opportunity becomes tantamount to mere virtue signaling. It's more of the same—admiring the problem.

True leadership diversity moves from being a passive initiative of targets to being a sustainable, action-filled initiative with better results for both diversity and performance—the two must go hand in hand for shareholders' sake—when there is a plan, a structure, a consistent process, and a commitment to being more diverse.

A commercial for Southern New Hampshire University in 2017 almost got it right. Their claim was "The world in which we live, equally distributes talent, but it doesn't equally distribute opportunity."[7] I believe it should have said "The world in which we live, equally distributes potential, but it doesn't equally distribute the opportunity to develop that potential."

Any organization that says they are *for* diversity but does not have a structured and measured approach to providing equal development among its diverse and underrepresented aspiring leaders is not really committed to diversity in its leadership ranks. *These organizations are in love with the concept of diversity, but not the practice of diversity.* And the practice of diversity is far more than just ensuring that the ranks are diverse at each level, or that diverse candidates have sponsors, or even that diverse candidates get opportunities to interview for promotional positions.

This is highlighted in the NFL's current struggle to arrive at true diversity among its head coaches, despite the adoption of the Rooney Rule in 2003. To be fair, the rule is not a complete failure because it did provide more opportunities for diverse coaches to be considered.

But the NFL is a microcosm of American business where winning is everything.

In any industry where performance is paramount but diversity is elusive, it's an unspoken admission that diverse candidates are not as developed, and therefore unprepared to step into these high-performance roles. The practice of diversity—if it's going to be more than virtue signaling—must include a coaching/mentoring program to help people *at all levels* prepare for the next couple of levels of upward mobility and increasing responsibility.

When employees (diverse or not) are installed in these positions of greater responsibility with the right behaviors, competencies, and skills, they can win with high-performance leadership and results—not just defined by short-term results, but over the long term.

WHITE MALES—AND EVERYONE ELSE

What happens to many minority executives? In their groundbreaking research for their 1999 book *Breaking Through*, David A. Thomas and John J. Gabarro found that there are two fast tracks in organizations: one for white males and one for women and minorities.

They found that white males tend to be selected early in their careers—in their twenties—and then given time to grow and take on more challenging assignments. Women and minorities, however, don't receive personal investment in their development until they reach their mid-careers—approaching their forties—often only after they have *proven* themselves to be worthy of investment.[8]

By then, with a much shorter career runway, the learning and development process takes on a protracted timeline as long-ingrained habits and behaviors become more difficult to change. Many run out of career before they can advance much further, and they feel stuck in mid-level management positions. They can easily become resigned to the notion that they are unable to rise toward senior executive-level positions.

Since good mentoring can take one to three years to yield meaningful results in style and approach to leadership, white employees on the fast track will have a runway of thirty years or more to make meaningful and increasing impact in their companies, whereas their minority counterparts will have career and impact trajectories for only fifteen or so years. According to Thomas and Gabarro, having strong mentors keeps minorities from giving up too soon.[9]

It's fairly easy to spot the fast-track people; they are more often than not white males who start getting assignments early in their careers. They tend to stay in these assignments for shorter periods of time than anyone else, get selected for other assignments, and so on.

At some point in most companies, these rising executives get the benefit of a coach, who is generally an external organizational development psychologist. This coach can give them any number of personality assessments and guide them through areas for development so that they learn to manage the things that can derail them or impede their effectiveness.

Every successful leader I've known readily admits that they succeeded because they got help along the way when others invested in them. It takes a trusting relationship and counsel and coaching from people much more senior to advance through a company's ranks. It also takes a person who is a willing and humble learner.

I believe formal mentoring should also take place at even higher levels of an organization, although it might take on different forms. The higher one rises, the easier it is to succumb to the echo chamber paradox, where the voices become more affirming and even patronizing, causing the leader to lose grounding and perspective.

It's never a bad thing to keep improving leadership effectiveness.

Proper mentoring helps the mentee see their aspirations and career goals in a framework and context of investments that require trade-offs regarding other goals and priorities and the time requirements to accomplish them. The process consists of discovery, coaching, teaching, and practice in order to enable the mentee to acquire and/ or refine their behaviors, competencies, skills, and perspectives necessary to succeed as an effective and trust-building leader.

Mentoring isn't about getting diverse people to think alike, but rather to get them to synchronize their perspectives—borne from their unique cultural backgrounds—with the mission, goals of the organization.

As such, this type of mentoring requires a safe space where transparency and vulnerability can abide. Leaders and emerging leaders who are equipped to listen to feedback, examine themselves introspectively, embrace change, and map out a path for transformation are far more likely to succeed than ones who are blind or indifferent to the effect they have on people in the organization.

This equipping starts when someone more senior and seasoned invests the time to help the mentee identify their true aspirations, recognize their strengths and derailers, and accurately see the opportunities for development. When embraced by the mentee, this type of mentoring can change the narrative arc of his or her career and, by extension, their imprint on an organization.

A BETTER APPROACH TO LEADERSHIP DEVELOPMENT

The opportunity for equal development—especially in early career—is key to developing a diverse bench of leaders. A mentoring program that supports developing diverse leaders must be open to all comers, where everyone has an opportunity to opt in for development.

While not everyone will successfully make the trip because of the required commitment from the mentee—and that's true for all people groups—everyone who earnestly desires the opportunity to lead should have an opportunity for development.

Promoting people to see if they have the leadership chops doesn't work. No matter who they are, people who can't lead well flame out early in their careers, rising to positions that foster broken cultures resulting in high turnover and poor performance.

Getting a diverse pool of candidates for any open position is a good start, but it doesn't guarantee success with sustaining diversity. If an employee's ultimate success is solely up to them, only the ones who figure out how to succeed in the organization can move forward. This can take an inordinate amount of time, as seen by the lack of diversity at higher levels in most companies.

Perhaps General Electric is the best example of how to train leaders for high performance. Entry-level leaders and management employees go through an intense five-year training and development program before being assigned to leadership positions. The program is so intense that only about 2 percent of attendees make it into leadership roles.

Using the annual performance review to coach employees is wholly inadequate for developing people. As a result, they flail around and often gravitate toward overusing their perceived strengths, which becomes a career-limiting effort.

Leadership development notwithstanding, most organizations also have a secret code for succeeding: the unwritten or unspoken rules for how to successfully and effectively navigate the organization in order to accomplish their goals. The uninitiated are often clueless, and with the best of efforts, they still fail because senior leadership didn't take them under their wing to show them how to succeed and maintain visibility.

Employers professing to embrace diversity through equal opportunity should certainly be interested in how many opportunities are presented to a diverse workforce. But equally important, these employers should also be measuring the percentage of underrepresented workers who are prepared, or preparing, to succeed at not just the next level but several levels upward.

Corollary to this point is the quantitative comparison of where diverse employees are in their respective careers. For example, if most of the candidates for any particular role are within five years of being out of school, but all the eligible diverse candidates are mid-career, the aspirations for a diverse workforce may not be achieved in any reasonable time.

If you subscribe to the notion that developing people for leadership is key to sustaining performance and developing people equally is key to building and sustaining diversity, then let's explore a concept of people development that is structured, intentional, and repeatable. Just freewheeling development or depending on employees who correctly self-report on development needs aren't going to provide the results you're looking for.

3

MENTORING CONCEPTUALIZED

*...Mentors and mentees [should] work together
for an extended period of time...[meeting] about
all aspects of leadership...*
—Ed Catmull

More than 70 percent of Fortune 500 companies report having a mentoring program of some sort.[10] These programs range from informal to highly formal, and from new-employee orientation to executive development.

Additionally, the corpus of mentoring books is full of tutorials on how to have an effective mentoring program. Each has a particular view of what it is and how to deploy it. Some even go so far as suggesting how to have a culture of mentoring within the organization. Across the literature, mentoring is viewed as developing others or helping others grow in one or more areas.

Although there are many differing concepts and constructs of mentoring, it is often conceptualized as a personal or professional relationship founded on trust and mutual respect for the purposes of exploring areas for development in which a mentee desires growth or a mentor sees an opportunity for growth. When applied formally in the context of an organization, it can be thought of as a form of facilitated leadership development, one-on-one or one-on-many. This is in contrast to the self-directed leadership development used in many, if not most, organizations.

Jim Collins makes the case in his book *Good to Great* that outcomes for any organization are inextricably tied to the leader and his or her capacity, style, and behaviors.[11] Organizational psychologists Zenger and Folkman corroborate this finding with their research and subsequent model as outlined in their book *Extraordinary Leader*.[12] Since the time that Bass and Yamarino began their research on leadership effectiveness in the 1960s and '70s, studies on leadership have proliferated, and all of them conclude that a leader has an undeniable effect on an organization's culture, performance, and results.

Leadership matters, and leaders matter. Bill Hybels, former senior pastor at Willow Creek in the Chicago area, was fond of saying, "When a leader gets better, everyone wins."[13] To get a different trajectory and better outcomes, in business and in life, a leader must first embrace change.

When leaders dare to embrace change in themselves, they make it safe for everyone else in the organization to embrace change. When change happens in leaders and their organizations, the outcomes and performance results are affected. The question is whether they are sustainable.

In poorly run companies that live by "results at any cost, attrition runs high, lack of trust exacts a tax on efficiency, and results cannot be sustained. In well-run companies, one can observe sustained results over a protracted period of time, with better margins and lower-than-average attrition.

The literature for professional development is rich, but there is rarely a structured approach that builds upon learned and applied competencies and concepts: Learn and apply this, and then learn and apply that.

Rather, these types of learning opportunities tend to be presented as stand-alone content modules—a smorgasbord of material to let the learner pick and choose what they want to learn or what they feel they need to learn.

As important as this is, one of the biggest problems with this approach, diversity notwithstanding, is that many employees base their development path on their own self-identified gaps, which are inaccurate and produce inadequate results. The research is clear that individuals are poor at self-reporting. Richard Nisbett and Timothy Wilson (1977) found that "we do not have access to the cognitive processes to help us understand what we do or why we do it."[14]

This is why self assessment and self–identification of developmental needs is inherently flawed and ultimately will not produce the desired outcome of getting to an equipped workforce at all levels—diverse or not. For anyone to select their own transformational development path with some measure of accuracy requires the input of one or more people who can help them accurately see the impediments to their effectiveness. That is the role of a mentor.

Leadership development is manifested in different ways. In many large companies, a library of professional development content and courses is available at the click of the mouse. Some companies have leadership development programs and courses with a one-size-fits-all approach to teaching and coaching. Everyone goes through the same curriculum at the same time and pace.

These courses are generally short-duration and specific to a leadership topic or principle. While the learning here can be highly informative, or even inspirational, this sage-on-stage approach can often miss the mark for individual discovery and development.

One can only become the best version of themselves when they are humble enough to get feedback or input from a mentor who has their best interest at heart and can make them aware of the behaviors, attitudes, and habits that hold them back. But it's not enough to learn what one is not doing well; a good mentor will also point the way to practices, skills, and competencies that will help the mentee gain more effectiveness as a leader. More effectiveness invariably leads to better results.

The mentor can also be a great accountability partner to help the mentee be thoughtful and intentional with decisions to change. When people become the best version of themselves, their careers can take on a new trajectory, and here the benefits of a diverse organization begin to emerge. The point of formal mentoring is to help the mentor be individualized with their coaching so that mentees will become meaningful and impactful contributors in a diverse organization.

Some companies recognize the value of mentoring, but many of these mentoring programs take on one of three manifestations: an ad hoc, as-needed approach for specific development needs identified by superiors; a mentee-selected mentoring approach (if the mentor is willing); and an everyone-is-a-mentor-to-someone approach, where those with the best relationships get the most mentoring attention.

Very few, if any, companies provide formal and structured one-on-one or one-on-few mentoring programs for all individuals who are interested in being developed. Ed Catmull, the cofounder of Pixar and former president of Walt Disney Animation Studios, understood this concept very well and implemented such a program in his own organization.

He paired new and young managers and leaders with senior and more experienced managers. In his words, "A key facet of this program is that mentors and mentees work together for an extended period of time—eight months. They meet about all aspects of leadership, from career development and confidence building to managing personnel challenges and building healthy team environments."[15]

DIVERSITY MATTERS

While there is still debate on the issue of whether diverse companies outperform nondiverse companies, financially, one point is nearly indisputable. Diverse companies—companies that more closely reflect society, from top to bottom—are more culturally sensitive and can successfully address population segments that others can't.

Development opportunities notwithstanding, diversity is often conceptualized as the outcome of having consistently provided equal opportunity for diverse people to apply for and interview for any given position.

The unspoken part of this, however, is that only a limited number will make the grade, and even fewer will rise to the next level. The ones who figure out the tacit organizational secret code are the ones who get selected, while the rest, competent as they may be, get left out.

The reasons the last four decades of diversity initiatives—through the likes of EEO and affirmative action—haven't substantially changed the outcomes at mid- and senior-levels across corporate America are two-fold.

First is that the interviewing and selection processes are flawed. Hiring managers are more likely to hire someone they are subconsciously comfortable with (i.e., someone who is most like them) and then justify the hire as someone that they are convinced will deliver the desired performance results based on previous performance.

Second, many underrepresented people groups don't receive the same development as employees who fit the dominant profile until much later in their careers.

WHEN DEVELOPMENT MEETS DIVERSITY

Some of the books on mentoring recognize the need for and the benefits of diversity in the workplace, but none of them has explicitly tied mentoring to building and sustaining diversity. To achieve and sustain a greater degree of diversity at all levels of an organization, leaders and emerging leaders have to be developed to successfully take on more and more responsibility.

This type of development comes best from more senior people who intentionally and purposefully spend time with a more junior person. A dear friend of mine, Dr. Billy Browning, who has been a highly successful organizational psychologist for more than forty years, observes that "those who are nurtured and coached in an organization mature and blossom."

Dr. Browning has seen this played out over and over as he worked with boards and C-suite executives of Fortune 100 companies, helping them build high-performance teams and change or mitigate the things that impede their effectiveness. The effects of personal investment by a more senior executive are not difficult to see, especially in larger organizations.

Companies that implement mentoring programs, no matter how formal or informal, must take care to not end up with a pool of mentees who learn to think like the leaders or mentors to get noticed or promoted. When this happens, the essence of what it means to be diverse is lost, and the culture becomes more and more homogeneous in thought with each successive level rising to the top of the corporation.

The concept for the corporation committed to diversity is the same as the genesis for our word *university.* Within the university, there is unity in diversity. But oneness should never be confused with sameness. There is a big difference between having a common vision and language—which are some of the elements that define an organization's culture—and thinking alike. Like the university example, when only one system of thought is accepted and all others subjugated to scorn or ridicule, oneness gives way to sameness and all real learning stops.

The point of having a common language is to have a shared syntax for describing problems, solutions, opportunities, and threats and to keep us from talking past each other. Companies that are committed to diversity are not afraid of a more fluid language, one where new terms, descriptions, and meanings are adopted and shared across the entire organization. Companies with a very rigid language can appear to be far more exclusive than inclusive and may therefore struggle with diversity at more senior levels.

However, I want to be careful to note that any new adaptations to language can arbitrarily change neither the objective nature of truth nor the essence of the organization's mission and vision. Truth, quite simply, is that which adequately defines reality. Adopting a new term that changes the nature of 2+2 to equal 3 is a very dangerous road for any organization.

A common vision is essential for a high-performance culture. Without it, the organization becomes dysfunctional and is fractured by misaligned or competing goals, the antithesis of high performance. It's easy to get caught up in an outcomes-based approach to diversity (egalitarianism), but that is attempting to fix the symptom, not the problem.

For many companies, fixing the symptom is easier, less expensive (at least in the short term), and takes far less time. It appeases the stakeholders but doesn't really address the underlying issue. As any good doctor will tell you, if you want to fix a medical problem, you must start with the root cause; don't treat the symptoms.

The Diversity Dilemma was written to provide a structure and a process for mentors to equip emerging and diverse leaders with a more effective toolset for effecting change and outcomes in the organizations they lead. This is accomplished through facilitated growth and development in a small group setting of diverse employees.

Noted psychologist Abraham Maslow once said, "If all you have is a hammer, the whole world looks like a nail."[16] If a leader has only one way to manage and lead, and it is filled with awareness gaps, their effectiveness (or lack thereof) becomes the limiting factor in their career trajectory, their organization's performance, or both. Similarly, if an organization views development needs uniformly across all its employees, its attempt at mentoring will be one-dimensional and likely miss the true development needs of each individual.

I believe that there are many senior executives who are in love with the *idea* of diversity, but not in love with the *work* of diversity. Executing a program of this nature with rigor and thoroughness, consistently over several years, will ensure the hard work of diversity sustains a diverse culture.

The structure presented in the following chapters lays out what I believe are the five elements of an effective developmental mentoring program: relationships, program structure, curriculum, mentee selection process, and mentors chosen.

4

WHOSE RESPONSIBILITY IS DEVELOPMENT?

The joy of leadership comes from seeing others achieve more than they thought they were capable of.
—Simon Sinek

My journey as a mentor of junior- and mid-level executives and emerging leaders for more than twenty years has been one of discovery and growth for me as well as my mentees. Having witnessed them go through their own process of discovery and growth, I've long been convinced that good mentoring can change a person's career and personal life trajectories.

But to do this effectively, the mentor and the material must meet every mentee right where they are. Every story is unique, and therefore every path to leadership effectiveness will be unique.

The point of mentoring as outlined in this book is that each mentee would emerge from the program with changed perspectives, behaviors, skills, and competencies, and as a result, a new trajectory for their leadership and career.

However, the premise of the book is that people will engage differently with the material; some will struggle in areas that seem obvious and easy for others. The path to get to the basics of effective leadership will likely be different for each person in the mentoring circle; therefore, the material must be broad enough to touch everyone right where they are.

DEVELOPMENT ISN'T ONE-SIZE-FITS-ALL

One of the most important insights I gained while leading young managers and executives through a yearlong mentoring program is that every person has a unique combination of wiring (nature) and experiences (nurture) that defines them as leaders. Because of this uniqueness, any mentoring program designed to bring people along to a healthy and effective leadership style must not be a one-size-fits-all approach.

If mentoring is merely a recitation by the mentor of their own path to the top, or a set of directions about things the mentee should know or be better at, it will likely miss the target of helping them accurately identify and embrace their own individual development needs. This "follow my path" kind of mentoring requires nothing but a few minutes here and there, and while some of the information may be helpful or even inspiring, it does little to impact the mentee.

Further, what passes for mentoring in some companies does little to really change the outcomes for the broader management/leadership team in a significant way, let alone have a meaningful impact on diversity.

WHY TIE DEVELOPMENT TO DIVERSITY?

While more people today support some form of affirmative action to help advance underrepresented groups in the workforce, according to Pew Research, the percentage of people who favor preferential treatment has not grown in more than thirty years. Many so-called diversity programs have a fundamental flaw in that they are based on preferential treatment toward people who fit into certain categories.

However, these types of affirmative action programs, and the ostensible opportunities they represent, have not yielded the results originally intended. This is due in large part to the fact that people may get preferential treatment in being selected, but if they don't get an equal opportunity to be developed toward highly effective leadership skills, succeeding in the job or beyond the job becomes much more difficult.

Preferential treatment, as a selection mechanism, is a subset of a larger problem when staffing an organization to improve productivity, innovation, morale, or outcomes. The larger problem is that any selection process that relegates merit and behaviors to the second, third, or fourth criterion will have an eventual negative impact on organizational performance and therefore, stakeholder value.

To be clear, *merit* is a proxy for predictably ensuring success in the role. It is not a proxy for accomplishment, experience, or even education. Companies and organizations that are committed to both performance and diversity need formal programs to coach or mentor their diverse candidates to be able to succeed by having the right leadership behaviors.

But whose responsibility is this type of mentoring?

MENTORING AS A CULTURAL IMPERATIVE

The current landscape of articles, seminars, and social learning modules is flooded with material on the benefits of diversity. David Livermore's book *Driven by Difference* highlights and draws attention to what is required to build cultural intelligence in an organization and encourage healthy debate among diverse perspectives. The question that must be answered by actions rather than by goal-setting and public pronouncements is this: *How do we sustainably build diversity into our organizations?*

Corporately mandated training courses on identifying and dealing with unconscious bias, raising diversity awareness, or initiatives that remind us of the importance of diversity are all important. But sustainable progress on diversity isn't made with more education and more awareness. Sustainable progress will be made when there is attention, intention, and programmatic effort on equal development, not just equal opportunity.

Most corporations that are committed to diversity have programs and policies designed to get a more diverse workforce. Sadly, many approaches to diversity are shallow and are employed for managing a preestablished outcome rather than solving the real problem. Some of these programs and policies are intended to help the company meet EEO or affirmative action quotas, real or perceived, or are used as evidence to sway public or internal perception of a company's commitment to diversity.

Unfortunately, too many leaders in corporate America still view diversity from the perspective of measuring the mix of headcount or the mix of the available pool of candidates. If the mix looks good, everyone is happy that the goals for diversity have been achieved. However, many diversity initiatives amount to nothing more than organizational enlightenment or virtue signaling with no tangible sense of purpose, direction, or qualitative goal in mind.

Despite all the enlightenment, many companies in Silicon Valley, for instance, still have a dilemma.

The Valley is arguably still a homogeneous work environment, and the problem is worse as one observes the more senior ranks of many high-tech companies.

In the tech world of Silicon Valley, the danger is that organizational enlightenment without an intentional and purposeful approach to helping diverse candidates succeed will only result in half-hearted attempts to appease shareholders, employees, and the public and not in any meaningful change in the most senior ranks of these companies.

At the time I was finishing this book, a major bank admitted that their diversity effort never amounted to anything more than giving diverse candidates a chance to interview, with little to no intention to hire them for key positions.

One of the problems of mentoring programs that aren't part of corporate culture and purposefully tied to building and sustaining diversity is that we will tend to default to our human instincts. We will tend to pick people most like ourselves to mentor, and as a result, the approach to problem-solving tends to be very homogenous as it is propagated through that part of the organization.

If you subscribe to the notion that leaders *can* be developed, the question for those who are already effective leaders is this: *Will you take the time to develop leaders—and especially diverse leaders? If not, then who will?*

Your answer to this question will determine whether your mentoring program will have any meaningful impact on diversity in the culture of your organization.

Further, how your organization defines and executes its mentoring/coaching/people-development programs will determine whether your company's culture and diversity programs will yield the desirable results of building and sustaining a diverse organization.

Here's the dilemma: If you leave your succession planning to a very Darwinian approach of survival of the fittest, nothing about your diversity profile is likely to change. If you pick leaders based on a profile, chances are that nothing about your organizational performance is likely to change.

The only way to avoid this dilemma is to institute a mentoring program that becomes part of the organizational culture for all levels of leadership. This requires commitment, modeling, attention, and inspection from the very top of the organization. This is not an HR mandate but rather a corporate value instilled by leadership.

HOW DO YOU KNOW YOU'VE SUCCEEDED?

Simply measuring diversity as a result or an outcome and expecting it to change is like running a business on only lagging indicators. But as any good leader in business will tell you, there are lagging indicators and leading indicators. Every quarter, earnings reports are delivered to the market to indicate how companies have performed, and these reports generally have influence over a company's stock price.

Good analysts, however, will pore over the financial statements to look for what should have been leading indicators of a company's performance so that they will have an expectation of the potential for the following quarter's performance.

It's not that lagging indicators are bad; they just can't be trusted to inform how or where to fix a problem. Rather than measuring the lagging indicators of diversity, there are some trusted leading indicators that will tell if an organization is making the right changes to its structure and processes to develop leaders equally.

When it comes to evaluating the health of an organization or performance relative to values, almost all leading indicators are behavioral. In other words, observing or measuring a behavior that directly affects a result is highly predictive of the outcome. Knowing how many diverse candidates have been hired to fill entry- and junior-level management positions is nice, but it is no more a predictor of diverse outcomes than measuring the number of employees from the country's top ten engineering schools is a predictor of technical innovation.

One litmus test for how well diversity—and by extension, inclusion—has taken root in the culture of any organization is the measure of how well a diverse perspective or viewpoint can be accepted, understood, and evaluated at all levels. This is especially important in light of the prevailing perspective and methodological leaning of the organization. Having diverse people on the team may not really make a difference if none are in key operational and strategy-setting roles. This is paramount to achieving diversity across the organization and up and down the organization.

If acceptance of diverse employees only amounts to tacit toleration but no real understanding of the value they bring to decision-making in key roles, then simply measuring ratios won't yield the kind of benefits that come from diverse cultures in problem-solving and innovating. No matter how it's measured (race, gender, beliefs, age, orientation, etc.), getting to a prescribed mix of employees doesn't really do anything unless there is diversity of thought manifested in a healthy discourse that ultimately unifies around a shared vision, mission, or purpose.

I'm not advocating for a plurality (multiple versions of vision, mission, or purpose) as the outcome for diversity here. Any company or organization that is divided on its vision, mission, or purpose will ultimately fail. Besides, the resources to pursue multiple paths to fulfilling any of those generally do not exist within well-run companies.

Diverse thought in an organization should result in a robust discussion, an examination of the data, and the pursuit of the best path to accomplish the mission—a path that may be often overlooked by homogeneity of thought and perspective.

True diversity is not just tolerance for each other, but rather acceptance and the necessary effort to listen to, understand, and entertain each other's points of view. No matter which side of any debate you're on, there is always another point of view worth considering. Simply having tolerance implies that "my point of view is right, yours is wrong, and I will kindly and tacitly hold to my own point of view while I politely listen to yours."

Real understanding suggests that "I have an opinion, but I am willing to listen to yours and work to understand it fully so that we can jointly evaluate the best path forward." This is the most certain way to demonstrate empathy for another's opinion and to honestly evaluate its validity for the solution that the team is working toward.

With all this said, the leading indicator of whether a company will succeed in its commitment to building and sustaining diversity is the diversity of the pool of people actively involved in developmental mentoring relationships. These are not freewheeling relationships, where every mentor determines their material and messages, but rather an organized and formal track of material to develop people with the leadership competencies and skills that are valued by and vital to the culture in the organization.

CULTURE TRUMPS STRATEGY

Any successful senior executive will tell you that culture trumps strategy any day. Because of this belief, these leaders own the culture of their organizations and take steps to promote and protect it. Noted psychologist Serge Moscovici (1988) held that cultures are defined by the traditions, symbols, rituals, objects, and language perpetuated by communication and stories within groups or cultures. This is true in society and in organizations.

A good mentoring program can be a vehicle for passing on to emerging leaders the organization's methodologies and language for evaluating ideas, prospects, processes, policies, and people—as opposed to just hoping people will catch on. This is the vehicle for conveying the common language and meaning of the important capacities, competencies, behaviors, and skills needed for effective leadership, as well as the vocabulary essential in identifying and discussing ineffective, minimizing, and disparaging leadership styles and behaviors.

In-house training programs can help with this, but self-directed online training and annual leadership gatherings and seminars designed to highlight thought leaders in particular areas do not have the same ability to effect change as a yearlong mentoring program. It is in these types of settings that competencies, behaviors, and skills are discussed, applied, and practiced with monthly readouts.

Without the ability to experience and practice the learning, Dee Hock, founder and former CEO of Visa, says that "our learning .... is forever crippled."[17] From top to bottom, and from silo to silo, the language must be straightforward and consistent. It is imperative that the important words, values, and beliefs of the culture must have the same meaning everywhere in the organization. A frontline manager, for instance, can't view accountability differently than the corporate executive on mahogany row.

Many organizational behavioral researchers readily acknowledge that organizations have a secret code for successful leadership. Without this code, aspiring leaders will flounder and fail to achieve their aspirations. Well-structured mentoring ensures that everyone knows the code for success and advancement, not just a select few.

Lastly, mentoring also provides a great vehicle for building strong relationships between aspiring leaders and senior-level executives. The body of research over the last two decades strongly indicates that mentoring, done well, is one of the factors that influence people's attitudes toward the workplace, and therefore, is a significant factor in whether or not people stay at companies. If you are interested in bending the curve on attrition, consider a well-developed mentoring structure to help people feel like they are valued.

While mentoring is not the only factor that keeps people engaged in the company, it certainly is one of the biggest contributors. Good mentoring helps employees feel like someone is taking an active interest in them and their careers.

HELPING LEADERS BECOME THE BEST VERSION OF THEMSELVES

Sometimes diverse candidates have the *ambition* to succeed but not the *tools*. Sometimes they must work harder than others to prove they have the chops. They have the willingness to work hard but are unaware of the path forward to succeed, or have the wrong picture of what success really looks like.

Just emulating the leader above them or their sponsor in the organization doesn't always work. Eventually, they and others around them discover that they've become someone else in order to get ahead. They may get short-term results, but changing who they really are does not have good long-term results for them or the organizations they lead.

If the path forward is just figuring out how to get this quarter's results or meet this year's expense budget, it's highly likely that there will be fallout, and for them, future advancement will become increasingly difficult.

As I mentioned at the onset, I wanted to be careful not to create a bunch of "mini-mes" through a development program. There is nothing more threatening to an environment of diversity than to staff an organization with people who all think alike, act alike, and view the world alike.

As Dee Hock once famously said, "Never hire or promote in your own image. It is foolish to replicate your strengths and idiotic to replicate your weaknesses. It is essential to employ, trust, and reward those whose perspective, ability, and judgment are radically different from yours."[18]

The same is true for developing people and is foundational to building a great mentoring program. Never attempt to develop in your own image.

The best path forward in an organization is for emerging and aspiring leaders to discover how to be the best version of themselves, to lead with authenticity, and to be acutely aware of the relationship between their own behaviors and the response of the organization. The most enduring way for them to acquire these kinds of tools is through the kind of mentoring discussed here: more than just information transfer, but one where the developmental needs and desires of the mentee are paramount to the relationship between mentor and mentee.

There has been much debate on whether leadership is nature versus nurture. The unspoken expectations of many organizations or their very senior leaders assume that leaders are born. But if leaders are born, then the goal of the organization should be to just test or assess employees until the ones with the right wiring are found and promote them.

The evidence found in well-regarded personality and leadership traits assessments—Myers-Briggs, Hogan Personality Inventory, and the Extraordinary

Leadership Model (Zenger and Folkman) among them—suggests something different. These assessments show that given accurate self-awareness of one's personal wiring and behavioral proclivities, and self-management coupled with a willingness to solicit and use feedback, people can develop into highly effective leaders. This makes effective leadership an act of the will coupled with uncommon humility, awareness, and feedback. To paraphrase a commercial for a popular online and distributed university, potential is evenly distributed, but the opportunity to develop that potential is not.

When a leader has the ability and courage to accurately see their leadership effectiveness and opportunities for growth, and can make the right behavioral changes, he or she can dramatically affect their corresponding operational outcomes. I have found through my own developmental programs that both one-on-one and small-group mentoring are highly effective for instituting the change necessary to alter outcomes across the organization.

While one-on-one mentoring is much more targeted to specific development needs of an individual mentee, small group mentoring—in groups of twelve or fewer people—has better short- to mid-term results for operational performance and long-term establishment of a bench of qualified candidates for increasing responsibility.

THE ESSENTIALS

How then does one go about putting in place a good developmental mentoring program? As a result of my own trial-and-error journey of assembling and developing this mentoring program, I offer some structure and ideas that have been effective over the last couple of decades and which include the input of some of the thought leaders in management and leadership effectiveness.

I believe this writing will provide some content and thoughts that you might consider in forming your own mentoring program. If you don't have a mentoring program, then feel free to use mine. The main thing is to have a consistent and repeatable structure and curriculum for your mentoring program—with values, expectations, and cadence—so that you can drive consistent results in personal and professional growth across a diverse set of candidates. At the same time, as my own experience corroborates, you'll improve your organization's performance.

Case in point: When I took over the leadership of a large field organization for a Fortune 50 company, the organization was in last place among five divisions in all three measures of success: financial, operational performance, and safety scores. After investing in the leadership structure to change the culture and mentor the first- and second-level leaders, the organization moved to first place in all three measures in under three years.

A great mentoring program has five essential elements:

1. It must have senior executive sponsorship.
2. It must have great mentors.
3. It must have a deployable, repeatable, and consistent structure.
4. It must have mentee commitment to the journey.
5. It must have an atmosphere of trust and collaboration, where mentees can learn from the mentor and from one another as they share their victories and struggles in their journey to become the best version of themselves they can be.

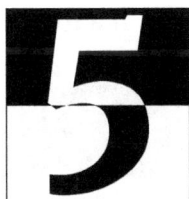

5 THE FIVE ESSENTIALS

Find a great mentor who believes in you; your
life will be forever changed.

—*Bill Walsh*

Patrick Lencioni, in his book *The Three Signs of a Miserable Job*, says that one of the top reasons people leave companies is that they feel that no one knows them.[19] Mentoring, done well, helps employees feel like someone knows them and takes an active interest in them. It also helps the employees know themselves, which may be even more important.

Lillian Eby et al. (2008) found that mentoring was significantly related to favorable behavioral, attitudinal, health-related, interpersonal, motivational, and career outcomes. The social psychologists whose research is focused on mentoring relationships generally observe that mentoring is one of the things that keeps people at companies. It also increases job satisfaction and leads to more frequent promotions and higher income. It's not the only thing, but it is one of the biggest contributors.

To do a formal mentoring program of this nature well, there are five essentials that must be addressed by the organization. Let's unpack them one at a time.

ESSENTIAL NO. 1: EXECUTIVE SUPPORT

I spent many of the last twenty-five years of my career doing *turnarounds*—that is, turning around organizations whose performance was lagging all comparable organizations, whether internal or external. Successful turnaround efforts always start with a diagnosis of what's broken in the culture. Until the culture is fixed, no attention to strategy, processes, or outcomes will have any real effect.

The point is that if formal mentoring (intentionally developing people) is not ingrained in the culture of the organization—as fostered, sponsored, or modeled from the very top—it will always be viewed as a program that can get paused or canceled with some organizational or operational emergency: this quarter's financial performance; the stock price; operations or performance push; or a change in the latest HR-led initiative to educate, train, and develop people.

At the time I had instituted the first formal mentoring program, I was less than a year into an assignment I had been given to turn the division around. Early on, I had recognized the signs of a broken culture and knew from experience that unless the culture got fixed, nothing else was going to make a difference in the outcomes. But changing the culture in a nine-thousand-person organization is far different than changing the culture in an early-stage company. I could have a personal impact and be accessible to the top two layers of management, consisting of fewer than fifty people. I figured that if I changed the culture at those levels and then spent time very visibly investigating and observing the culture at the working level, culture change would happen much more rapidly.

The opportunity to begin investing in the top two layers of management came with the formal mentoring program. I realized that I couldn't have scripted a better way to change the culture in such a large organization.

The program started such a stir that virtually everyone in those two layers was waiting expectantly for an opportunity to participate in the program. Since the groups were not larger than twelve people, it took three and a half years—I ran the last two groups concurrently, but staggered by six months— to get everyone through the program. But the impact on the organization and the culture began to happen before the end of the first circle, as leaders began to learn from each other, and I used some of the topics in presentations for quarterly meetings at the various offices of the division. In the end, people understood my commitment.

When viewed only as a *"nice to have,"* a formal mentoring program will always be an adjunct to organizational activity rather than central to it. Earlier, I discussed the importance of culture to an organization. Kim Cameron (1997), in his research on organizational culture, found that easily three-quarters of strategic planning, reengineering, cost-cutting, and total quality management efforts fail because they didn't first address the cultural changes needed to succeed.[20]

CULTURE

Culture—as Cameron, Serge Moscovici (1988), and others found—is defined by norms, traditions, common language, assumptions, and behaviors.[21] These characteristics are modeled and exemplified by the very top of the organization first. If not, the organization never really develops a deep culture that affects its performance. Without making a formal mentoring process part of the culture, there is a very high likelihood that it will fail or at least fizzle out.

This notion is especially important when it comes to mentoring as the vehicle to develop and sustain a diverse workforce. Senior executives in any organization have a thorough understanding of the behaviors, skills, competencies, and cultural understanding necessary for success in key leadership positions.

When they work with HR leaders to map these success characteristics and behaviors to a development program open to all aspiring and emerging leaders in the organization, a more representative pool of candidates for key leadership positions will emerge.

By doing this and showing the executive commitment to this institutionalized development program, underrepresented people groups will get a clear message that this is not just another diversity initiative but rather a change in how the organization addresses the very real predicament of having too few diverse candidates in the pool of candidates for key leadership positions.

ESSENTIAL NO. 2: REMOVING THE BARRIERS

I describe these barriers from the perspective of a senior executive with expense budget pressure and operational goals to meet. It's also viewed through the lens of the psychology of organizational resistance to the process and the corresponding personal resistance to change. I also offer some guidance on how to recognize these barriers—organizational, personal, and psychological—and institute the necessary policies to ensure the long-term viability of a mentoring program of this nature.

Formal mentoring programs that make a difference to both the culture and the performance of the organization do not come without costs or obstacles. Without the prevailing and persistent commitment of senior executives, the costs of letting people travel for face-to-face meetings, executive time away from solving thorny operational issues, and so on, all become potential obstacles to sustaining and maintaining a formal mentoring program.

SELECTING MENTEES

The first barrier to success is the selection process. The inclination for leaders in the organization is to select the "most deserving" people, or those with the greatest perceived potential, first. The problem here is that perceptions of potential or deserving can be inherently and unconsciously biased. This overlooks people's desire and commitment to learn and develop. Unfortunately, this is exactly how many "mentoring" initiatives materialize and why diversity appears to diminish the higher one rises through the ranks in most organizations.

One lesson for me as a mentor is not to prejudge anyone's potential or development needs until I get more information. Early in my career, I learned a lesson from my mother-in-law that I never forgot: "If you knew just one more fact about someone, it would change your opinion." That lesson has kept me from prejudging people on several occasions—and consequently from limiting someone's opportunity to prove themselves.

This should inform how we select people for development in an organization. It's true that not everyone will "make the trip," but that's not the point. Everyone should be able to opt in (audition), and the program should be structured to give everyone the attention of a coach who can develop their talent. If you try to pick the "winner" up front, you'll likely be surprised, and the consequences of this could be that a great leader gets overlooked and never gets to make a significant contribution to the organization.

During my time leading this program, I have been surprised on more than one occasion by mentees who exceeded any expectations I had of their potential.

Case in point: We met Janet earlier in this book. She is the young lady who inspired me to begin this program. After struggling in place for several years, she finally acquired the skills to succeed at more senior levels, and in the years since her involvement in the program, she has been promoted at least five times. In the most recent communication I received from her (she has kept me up to date on her career for the last six or seven years), she had been promoted to vice president of her company.

A better way to view this process is to consider ambition, desire, and eagerness to learn while assembling a pool of mentees who represent a good cross-section of the employee base, without being intentionally skewed toward any one people group.

PSYCHOLOGICAL FRAMEWORK

The second barrier to success is the psychological framework of the mentees. It's been my experience that junior executives are often nervous that their involvement in a mentoring circle will be interrupted by their boss, or boss's boss, due to a conflicting priority. These conflicts generally come in the form of an operational exigency.

Further, some have a "tape" that plays in their head that works against their own success. That tape plays when making decisions, interacting with customers or employees, or receiving feedback from others. It tells them they're not worthy, that they're not good enough or smart enough, that they will be ridiculed, or that they'll do it wrong, setting themselves up for criticism.

Sheri, one of the early members of a mentoring circle, said, "There were so many impactful moments, but suddenly I caught myself arguing with the negative tape that plays in my head. Then it hit me—I've become aware of the negative tape, and I see how allowing it to continue to play has held me back. The negative tape says: *'I could have done more. I could have done it better than I did. I should have said this instead.'* That unhelpful self-talk led me to shy away from going too far outside my comfort zone. I thought I was working on improving, but I was actually just going over the same old ground.

"It's not about picking myself back up. It's about playing a tape that is more realistic and empowering.

I can get better without the negativity. I thank you for this realization since prior to your discussion on the tape that plays, I did not even know mine was harmful."

The point is that an environment of psychological safety, where people are free from tension and can experience change, is paramount to a successful mentoring experience. Further, when the mentee must continually abide by the potential of conflicting priorities, their level of engagement is only a fraction of others who can lean in and give themselves fully to the group, the material, and the process. Commitment to change will be directly proportional to the level of engagement of each mentee. As people are, by nature, resistant to change, any psychological framework that makes it easy for people *not* to change becomes an enemy of the program.

THE COST OF MENTORING PROGRAMS

The third barrier to success is finances. Well-run organizations are led by people who are fully aware of the financial performance of their company or organization. As such, they make wise financial decisions and have good accountability practices to ensure that decision-makers have the right framework for making sound financial decisions.

Having a formal mentoring program that meets face-to-face every month is a financial commitment. This needs to be baked into the operating costs of the organization. Otherwise, when a push comes to hold or reduce quarterly expenses, the expenses associated with the mentoring program can be cut. It's better to have a plan, when this happens, to move the mentoring circle a month, but establish a definitive date when it will be held. Indefinite postponement of the meeting only sends a message that the circle is not important and, by extension, that the investment in the people in it is not important.

One way leaders try to skirt this issue is by making the justification to meet virtually. On the surface, this seems like a reasonable decision. However, as a media psychologist, I understand well the things that are lost in a virtual meeting. Marshall McLuhan, the sociologist who authored *The Medium Is the Message*, showed that with every new technology, something is gained but something is lost as well.

In virtual meetings using video-meeting technology, convenience and expense savings are gained, but attention, connection, and engagement are lost, or at least reduced.[22] This has a deleterious effect on the purpose of the meeting: encouraging people to connect and lean in order to internalize the material and learn from each other.

EFFECTS ON PERFORMANCE

A successful and well-run mentoring program has a tangible effect on organizational performance and, therefore, financial performance.

When I first rolled out this program, I was turning around a large organization that had been perennially in last place among its peer group. Part of my effort was to lead in such a way as to change the culture. But I also knew that unless I grew a more effective leadership team, we might not make the turnaround.

After rolling out this mentoring program to groups of second-line managers, I began to see a difference in our performance metrics before the second group was finished with its yearlong track. Over time, I could see that our trajectory of performance had markedly changed, which made the return on investment easy to measure. To the point I made earlier—the program was becoming part and parcel of the culture itself. As it turned out, the more our operational metrics and financial performance changed, the more I wanted to invest in the program. I did this by running concurrent and overlapping mentoring circles during the year.

TYRANNY OF THE URGENT

The fourth barrier to success is the unfortunate timing of operational emergencies. Every company I've been associated with has had some sort of organizational push for end-of-quarter production and revenue, solving a customer problem, reacting to or recovering from a vendor failure, software failure, or natural disaster. To be fair, often these should take priority over everything else going on inside the organization.

But as with financial priorities, there should be a plan in place with a date certain for the next meeting so that the mentoring circle is done in a year from the start. Otherwise, this will tend to drag on, get postponed, and then a yearlong program turns into eighteen to twenty-four months. This can be discouraging to those who are making a personal commitment to the program and have an expectation that it will run for one year.

ESSENTIAL NO. 3: GETTING THE RIGHT MENTORS

Simon Sinek makes the point that due to changing societal norms and generational differences, the job of shaping younger generations into competitive and high-performing employees who could be future leaders is falling more and more to corporations.[23] This makes the role of mentors even more important today than in years past.

Getting the right mentors is foundational to building and sustaining a quality mentoring program that changes an organization. Formal mentoring programs are most effective when great care is given to the selection of mentors. These should be people who can be open to those they mentor and be aware that the very selection process can unwittingly signal bias—or at least preference—to the rest of the organization. Further, good mentors need to be willing to invest in people. It's more than just information transfer, but the relationship must foster personal change.

One of my mentees wrote to me several years after our time together. For Kerry, one of the most significant by-products of the mentoring process and the culture change that followed was that long after I had left the organization, she would see managers or technicians while in the field, and they would ask about me and tell stories about the culture that had been established. To them, the culture encouraged the team to want to contribute and be part of something bigger than themselves.

"That is a legacy we all should strive to achieve," she told me.

I certainly don't want the reader to think that I was the ideal mentor, or that I was perfect. The point is that the right mentors will have a ripple effect across the organization as they impact not only the people they directly invest in but also people who are two or three levels removed.

When employees perceive that their opportunity for development is disadvantaged by the way mentors relate to people, momentum around affecting diversity is undermined. Left unaddressed, emerging leaders in underrepresented people groups will begin to look for opportunities elsewhere, leaving the organization even more homogenous. The long-term effects are deleterious to having and growing a diverse leadership bench.

MENTOR CHARACTERISTICS

To be a great mentor in this type of program, one must be able to identify and rise above his or her perceptions and unconscious biases to see the value and potential in all people. It takes uncommon humility to resist the tendency to choose the familiar.

Several characteristics make good mentors. The first is that they must have a passion for developing people. Many times, I have seen senior leaders believe that their own success warrants passing on their tips and personal path to the top by way of a mentoring circle. However, this type of mentoring does not ensure success for the mentee and may even work counter to the goals of the type of mentoring program proposed by this book: building sustainable diversity at all levels of the organization and, with it, sustainably improved operational results.

Most leaders will agree with the *idea* of developing people, but not commit to the *hard work* of developing people. It's easier to develop clones—"Do what I did and think like I think"—than it is to make individualized investments in people to help them be the best version of themselves.

INVESTING IN PEOPLE

Directing people to the developmental materials available through a company learning platform is not enough. To make individualized investments in people, a mentor must get to know his or her mentees—their background, their perspective, their struggles, the obstacles they've overcome.

People will neither overcome their leadership deficiencies nor discover and overcome their blind spots without a courageous mentor to guide them, and the annual performance review is neither the time nor the place to start this process. I would advocate that among the criteria for moving into the senior ranks of a company should be willingness, ability, and demonstrated personal commitment to mentor others in a structured program of this sort.

The long-term benefits of a mentor who takes the time to invest in people at a personal level include modeling a behavior that gets passed on to future generations of employees.

One of the quieter and more introverted mentees that came through the program, Thomas, shared with me a number of years later the importance of investing in people like him. He wrote: "I can tell you that being part of the mentoring program...has been priceless. There have been many things that I have kept close as takeaways from that experience...You are the only leader of the business who took time to invest in me personally...I do all that I can to follow your lead and work to invest in my team at every opportunity."

COMPASSION

In addition to having a passion for developing people, great mentors must also have a genuine compassion for people. It would seem like this should follow, but it's much easier said than done. We all know that it's easier to demonstrate compassion for the people we really like than it is for the folks who rub us the wrong way. And this is where good mentors must take the time to get to know their mentees.

Having a love for people means that a mentor, like a good parent, wants to see everyone win. Whether or not they do is not entirely up to the mentee, as we'll see in the next section.

PRIORITIES MATTER

The next characteristic of a good mentor is the willingness to prioritize time apart from operational responsibilities to develop people. Part of leading people well is to make sure that everyone gets the support they need to change, grow, and become better versions of themselves. It's good for the people, and it's good for the organization. A formal mentoring program of the sort we highlight in this book indeed takes time and can easily get relegated to a position of unimportance, given all the demands on an executive's time. I know firsthand that it takes a purposeful effort to prioritize and devote the time to effectively mentor people.

MENTORS ARE LEARNERS TOO

Every time I led a mentoring circle, something happened that I never expected. I learned something that made me better in the next circle. I believe that one of the defining characteristics of a good mentor is the willingness and openness to learn. I look back through the notes I made with each mentoring circle, and I see where I learned something about what the mentees desired that I had overlooked.

I also see where I learned something about myself or my delivery of the material. Each time I made notes, they were folded into the workbook I used in subsequent mentoring circles. Even today, as I take another group through the material—almost ten years after I led the first circle—I find myself taking notes and making changes to the workbook to make it more impactful.

As of the writing of this book, more than ten years after the first mentoring circle, I'm mentoring a new generation of young business professionals. I still find myself learning from them, learning how to deliver the material more effectively, and tweaking the course to suit the needs of the mentees.

SOCIAL INTELLIGENCE

As I think about the top characteristics of a good mentor, it should include the leaders who show up where people are and connect. In one of the turnarounds I was responsible for leading, I found that people had rarely or never seen the former leader of the organization. No one can effectively lead an organization by driving their desk. This was a big part of the problem and one of the reasons I was asked to lead the division.

In my management-by-walking-around (MBWA) style of leadership, I determined to be in as many places as I could be in my first year, which subsequently carried over to the next year, and then the next. When it came time to roll out the first mentoring circle, and for successive circles, there was no end to the people who wanted to be in the group.

They knew me, and for as much as I could with the time I had, I knew them enough to begin understanding the real development themes and needs that junior leaders had. Almost every one of them had a good heart and really wanted to succeed with their organization; they just weren't equipped properly and didn't know how to cross that bridge. When leaders "show up" and become real to people in the organization, they establish a platform to invest in their leaders.

VULNERABILITY

When the mentors for a formal mentoring program are carefully selected and vetted for their character, commitment, and behavioral characteristics, the program will have the best opportunity to succeed.

Many times, we don't mentor others because we feel like we have nothing to contribute to someone else's journey or trajectory. Nothing could be further from the truth. It does take a few core characteristics, but our view of the richness of our own experience may have little to do with whether or not we can add value to someone else. It first takes a willingness to be vulnerable with our lives, enough so that people can learn from our mistakes, victories, failures, and successes.

INTEGRITY

It's very difficult to learn anything from people who can't admit they have ever made a mistake. The core characteristics of a good mentor start with integrity. Ross Perot had a philosophy that if a person cheated on their spouse, they would cheat on their expense report. He looked for nonobvious clues as to a person's character.

People in organizations have a way of figuring out who has integrity and who doesn't. People make sense of their lives and careers by telling stories. Stories connect us and are powerful tools in communicating values, passing on traditions, and framing people— especially senior leaders. Stories in dysfunctional organizations often frame leaders in unfavorable ways and almost always highlight the areas of their lives and leadership style that show a lack of integrity.

When leaders are admired and respected, these stories almost always highlight the deeds and actions that are examples of integrity, compassion, or resolve.

Without integrity, trust cannot be built, and without trust, people will not engage and learn in a mentoring experience.

People whom we desire to mentor will look for the clues that tell them whether there is consistency in our character. Inconsistencies speak to issues of integrity, and once that is gone, it's difficult to command respect. Others won't have respect for us as leaders, for our experience, or for any advice or counsel we would offer in a mentoring relationship.

Good mentors should also have a teachable spirit. This means that a good mentor must also be in the process of transformation. A leader's role is to take people from point A to point B. Groups that never need to grow, perform, or improve really don't need a leader. Going from point A to point B requires change or transformation. If a mentor can't embrace change, how will he or she ever get a mentee to embrace change?

As a mentor, it's difficult to take people to a place you haven't been yourself. When leaders or mentors stop growing and stop changing, they lose their effectiveness not only to lead but to speak into anyone else's life about the necessity for change.

DON'T ADMIRE THE PROBLEM

Having spent more than forty years in the corporate world, I have been in countless leadership seminars sponsored by the company I worked for, where world-class thought leaders such as Liz Wiseman, Sheila

Heen, and a host of others have spoken about their own research and findings.

At the end of these talks, panels of senior leaders are assembled onstage in panels to talk about how we should make a pivot here, how we could do things differently there, or how outcomes might be different if we would make this change. It's all well-intentioned, but afterward, we all return to our normal state of operation, and nothing really gets implemented. This is how we admire the problem.

We're all pretty good at highlighting the issues in the light of new concepts and information, but admitting that we got it wrong and that we've changed things is too difficult for the ego and may even be viewed as a sign of weakness. No one ever got up and said, "I really failed my people in this one area. Here are the changes I made, and here's what happened!"

Sadly, I would come away from these events, and within six to twelve months, almost everything that was talked about was forgotten and never really implemented. Highly successful people in organizations come away with the notion, "I got to where I am by doing what I'm doing, I'm not changing my recipe for success." And the tacit message received by the organization from the leader is this: "I'm just fine, but you have to change." It is in this context that most mentoring programs take place.

One of my favorite leaders, Bill Hybels, was often fond of saying, "When a leader gets better, everyone wins."[24] And it's true. When leaders see no need to change themselves, they will not be able to model change for their organization and for the people they mentor. Again, the essence of mentoring is to help others see the need for change and commit to change for the betterment of themselves and the organizations they serve.

LEAVE YOUR COMFORT ZONE

Lastly, mentors need to be able to leave their comfort zones. Great mentoring doesn't necessarily take place from a position of strength but from a position of humility. Mentoring from a position of strength looks like the mentor telling the mentee what to do and how to do it. It becomes almost an academic exercise.

Mentoring from a position of humility is being vulnerable and letting others see that the pain, struggles, obstacles, and lessons we've learned in our journey are the things that most affect our lives. It is also letting mentees have access to all that is rich about our own stories, for it is in these stories that they find inspiration.

One stoic mentee named Mike got the point of stepping out of one's comfort zone. He said it best this way:

> *"I joined [the] mentoring group in 2016 [and] my first assignment was to write my life's story as a narrative arc with me as the protagonist. The expectation was that I make myself vulnerable, exposing*

both successes and failures that led me to that point, and the story as I saw it to the conclusion of my life. I came to realize that this task was not only to expand my vision of myself out of the immediate and into the larger picture of what I wanted for my life, but also to help prepare my mind for the rest of the learning I would receive through this program."

What are you doing to inspire the leaders who will come after you? Or are you hoarding your experience, knowledge, and organizational power until the decision is made to replace you?

ESSENTIAL NO. 4: WHO SHOULD BE MENTORED?

The selection processes for those to be mentored vary widely in the available literature. Some advocate for the top 20 percent of performers; some advocate for mentees to select the person by whom they desire to be mentored; while others believe the process should begin with a mutual selection between the mentor and the mentee. One of the greatest departures of this book from the rest of the field is in the selection of those who will be mentored.

Just as in selecting good mentors, humility needs to be a hallmark of mentees worth investing in. I've heard, "It's just my nature to lead!" from aspiring young leaders as I've tried to coach them. This sort of exclamatory remark often puts an emerging leader at odds with any development effort that could increase their effectiveness and boost their organization's performance.

While it's true that dominant and extroverted personalities are often associated with leadership, several studies show that the world of highly successful senior leaders is split almost evenly between extroverts and introverts. There may be more visible leadership qualities in some than in others, but effective leaders can be developed and can come from a range of personality types.

Dominant personalities that aren't molded and nurtured can become bullies or control freaks. They are not authentic or effective leaders, and they do not prepare others to step up and lead either. Best-case scenario, because of their bruising and bloviating personalities, they may produce short-term results but have little to no sustainable effectiveness at all.

Further, they do not develop the next generation of effective leaders. This results in exacting a very high cost to the organization as measured in low employee morale, ineffective collaboration, time to innovate / time to market, low trust, or high attrition.

Building and sustaining diversity simply does not work when there are mentees in the group whose egos won't allow them to learn the tough lessons.

PREDICTING SUCCESS

Television shows like *The Voice* and *American Idol* are highly instructive about the selection processes for mentees. The top three lessons from these shows are: (1) Talent can be developed and refined; (2) raw talent alone doesn't ensure that one will get to the finals without the investment of a good coach and the willingness on the part of the contestant to learn; and (3) we should never judge a book by its cover.

It is nearly impossible to predict who will win just by watching the auditions. It's true that not everyone will make the trip, but that's not the point. As broad an audience as possible should be able to opt in (audition), and the program should be structured to give everyone the attention of a coach who can develop their talent. If you try to pick the "winner" up front, you'll likely be surprised.

Unfortunately, this is exactly how many mentoring initiatives materialize and why diversity appears to diminish the higher one rises through the ranks in most organizations. While the lesson we get from these TV shows of not prejudging people and their developmental needs is paramount to success in this mentoring program, we often overlook one important aspect of the shows: the contestants' willingness to learn from their coaches.

LOOKING FOR COMMITMENT

It's often difficult to assess the psychological framework through which a mentee approaches a formal mentoring program. As important as the mentors and the executive support are, the program can't succeed if the mentees don't commit to leaning in, learning, and applying newfound leadership skills and competencies. Janet, whom we met earlier, not only made it her mission to learn from and apply the lessons, but she also wanted to ensure the learning and sharing continued well after the yearlong mentoring circle. She arranged for the group to continue to meet once a month via videoconferencing so that her fellow mentees could continue to share their experiences.

In the mentoring groups I led, it was easy to see who was going to benefit the most from the circle. As much as I tried to make sure each mentee was committed to the process, not everyone had the same level of commitment. A couple of times, people dropped out because they realized they just weren't able to make the level of commitment necessary to profit from their time in the circle. Hard as this is, mentors must ensure that each mentee begins the mentoring circle with the intent to make the commitments and put forth the effort needed to become a more authentic and effective leader.

When I started the mentoring circles, I created a contract of sorts with each mentee. These mentees were selected by regional directors—I had no say in who would be in the group—as the people who most deserved a chance to be developed.

The first meeting was always a virtual meeting (videoconference or conference call) so that I could outline the process, explain the level of effort required, and give them the first assignment. At the end of the call, I asked each person who wanted to go forward in the mentoring circle to email me their commitment to be an active participant, make every effort to attend, and do the work necessary. Only a few times did people email me that they would be dropping out for one reason or another.

The selection process for mentees is critical for advancing diversity in the organization. Some mentoring books advocate picking the top 20 percent of emerging leaders as the ones worthy enough for personal investment. This process relies heavily on past performance as the measuring stick. For the same reasons I identified earlier—that we tend to pick people most like ourselves—this almost ensures a homogeneous pool of candidates for leadership positions. This does nothing to further the cause of getting to a diverse culture.

ESSENTIAL NO. 5: THE RIGHT STRUCTURE

Mentoring programs without the right structure may fail to focus on the individual's needs, desires, and intent and will only serve to exacerbate the problems in leadership transitions between generations and among diverse candidates. The structure of formal mentoring should support developing excellence in leadership and building diversity. It should also include a curriculum and learning process that allows mentees to learn and apply in increments as they reflect on their own leadership gaps and development.

As with any corporately sponsored program, structure is necessary to ensure consistent outcomes. While there is nothing sacred about the structure I propose here, the reader may want to use this as a model to develop a structure that better fits their organization and the geographical, financial, or operational constraints they have and to which the entire organization adheres. Too much variation in the structure across the organization will only serve to dilute the efforts and provide inconsistent outcomes.

CADENCE

The cadence of the program—monthly meetings for three to four hours—was laid out to allow for the time required for assignments, reading, writing, practicing newly learned behaviors, and getting feedback from the right people. In the types of organizations I led, the quarterly performance of operating units was expected and highly scrutinized.

Because of this visibility, we made the schedule for our monthly meetings such that any end-of-the-month push for results would not be a source of schedule conflict. Further, we also had a contingency plan for when we would meet on the outside chance we could not get together as originally planned. Over the course of seven mentoring circles, we had to move our monthly mentoring meetings only twice because of an end-of-quarter push that required people's full attention.

Every month, we met in facilities—offices, conference rooms, etc.—where we could keep operational distractions away from the meeting. For the duration of the meeting time, which generally included lunch, the entire group was focused on the discussion and learning. I asked all the mentees to silence their phones and not check emails, but made sure that we had a couple of breaks for people to check their messages and respond to urgent matters.

BUILDING GROUP TRUST

In a yearlong mentoring process, it's important to get the right start with a session that facilitates trust and camaraderie within the group and that each lesson builds on the previous one. The reader may elect to make some changes to this to fit your intended outcome; however, make sure that the series of lessons does not appear as a disjointed set of lessons with no connection from one to the other.

Since each lesson involved a required reading assignment, I made sure that I supplied all the books and other reading material. The list of books can be found in the bibliography of the curriculum.

With all the structural and environmental elements in place, we turn our attention to the curriculum, designed to build into each mentee the tools necessary for a career of feedback, honest self-reflection, change, and development. As their accuracy grows in identifying these gaps, they'll know which courageous steps to take to increase their effectiveness and enlarge their sphere of influence.

In the context of the reading and writing assignments, there is accountability among the mentees that helps them grow in the areas that have held back or even derailed their leadership in the past.

6 CURRICULUM

> *Tell me and I forget. Teach me and I may*
> *remember. Involve me and I learn.*
> **—Benjamin Franklin**

For the reader, I have two pieces of advice when reviewing the following curriculum that I used and still use, albeit with a few modifications.

First, consider the level of your mentees. While this course was designed for frontline managers and junior executives, you may find that some of the material can be better served as a review of things a more senior executive should already know or do (although in my experience, a frightening number of senior executives completely ignore these principles).

I have proposed a curriculum and cadence that takes a full year to complete. The mentoring process you use can be shortened or lengthened to suit the level and needs of the organization. I have found that giving mentees a full month to read a book, practice the featured or emphasized behaviors, and maintain their operational performance and priorities makes for optimal development. You may find otherwise.

Second, as a mentor, it is important to personalize the material by finding stories and examples from your own life and career to reinforce important points. As you'll see in Month One of the curriculum, we connect to stories. You're welcome to borrow any of my stories, but your stories of successes and shortcomings are an important part of the growth process and highly instructive for the decisions your mentees will face later.

MEET RHETT

One of my mentees, Rhett, was already a good leader in our organization when he entered the mentoring circle. But the one thing he lacked to become great was vulnerability, which would build trust with his employees.

At the end of our year together, Rhett wrote the following to me:

> *"After taking time to reflect on our journey together, the story that I prepared for our second meeting had the most impact on*

me and really set the tone for the group dynamic.

"Even though I knew that one of the goals of the story was to get us to open up and be vulnerable, I can say without hesitation that I did hold back a bit. I was worried about putting too much of myself out there and potentially being judged.

"As a result of our time together and listening to others' stories, I was inspired to be more vulnerable with others and allow them to see what makes me who I am. It's clear to me how much of an impact this can have on building trust and transparency!

"I really enjoyed getting to know my peers on a deeper level after that first face-to-face meeting where we all shared our stories. Additionally, as I shared with you, it really started a positive dialogue with my wife about what the 'front porch view' looks like. We continue to discuss this, and I can't stress enough how impactful the story exercise has been."

THE CURRICULUM

This curriculum, outlined here but expanded in *The Diversity Dilemma Workbook*, was refined over the first five years of use and has served me well, having led almost two hundred mentees through it.

I continue to tweak it based on the needs of the mentoring circle. It includes material from people I considered to be thought leaders in one or more areas of personal and professional development and effectiveness. There is nothing magical or sacred about the material I have assembled here. In all the leadership development material I have been through in my career and studies, as well as my own personal experience and observations over a forty-three-year career, there are a few principles that are enduring when considering the development of effective leaders and executives. The material I use continues to stand the test of time. It is as relevant today as it was in my first mentoring circle.

Whether you're leading a project team, a department, a division, or a company, these principles apply. To be effective, one must be willing to be introspective about their own behaviors, relationships, and style and to commit to personal and professional change needed to build trust, engagement, and inspiration across the organization. For these reasons, the material I have assembled has been highly instrumental in assisting me and those I have mentored on our journeys to be the best leaders we can be.

CHANGE IS NECESSARY

Mike, the one thing that had the most impact for me over this past year is my willingness to accept change. I have spent my twenty-

two-plus-year career in network services, intentionally unwilling to be open to new areas of interest, jobs, departments, or opportunities.

[Since our mentoring circle], I have changed my approach. I am actively seeking out change. I have immersed myself in [learning], specifically about software-defined networking and achieving a Big Data certification. Charting out my path from where we are to where we want to be (my story) was the biggest motivating factor in broadening my horizons and looking outside of my comfort zone.

For that inspiration, thank you. I would also like to thank you for the candid discussions, your time, and providing the platform for me to bond with my peer group. Each member of the group has something to offer that I would have otherwise not been exposed to. The sharing of knowledge and the support have truly been a blessing.

These were the words of Sunny, speaking of his own experience in the mentoring circle and confronting change in his own life.

It's important to understand that professional development must include some personal development for two reasons. The first is that personality assessments and research show that we are basically the same in private, or at home, as we are in the office or other professional settings (unless there is a sociopathic disorder of some sort).

The second is that for leaders who want to be better, change is mandatory. We must be willing to change to be the kind of leader who builds trust and makes it okay for others to embrace change. Since all change is personal, even for the highly trained and dispassionate professional, unless the *person* accepts and embraces change, the *professional* has little hope of enduring the kind of change needed to lead well.

A leader may mandate change for everyone else, and even feign change in professional settings to get everyone to follow suit, but organizations are good at detecting false pretense and manipulative behavior. For these two reasons, it's absolutely necessary for there to be an element of personal change in any curriculum involving professional change.

You may decide to use different material in your mentoring circles, but if so, don't lose sight of the principles I enumerated earlier. Leaders who take on an attitude of "This is who I am, take it or leave it" rarely, if ever, rise through an organization to become the people who drive change and produce lasting results in an ever-changing marketplace.

The following is a summary of the twelve-month curriculum for the mentoring circle. An expanded version of each month with examples, stories, discussion points, clarifying questions, and assignments, each with a call-to-action, can be found in the workbook.

MONTH ONE: WELCOME!

Your time is limited, so don't waste it living someone else's life.
—*Steve Jobs*

To get started on the right foot, it's important to get everyone onboarded with the right perspective and mindset. It's also important that everyone in the group hears the same words from me at the same time.

To accomplish this, we begin the year with a hosted conference call—the only meeting that is not face-to-face—with all the mentees who signed up and were recommended by their respective supervisors to participate.

On this call, I give a high-level overview of the program and curriculum and the expectations for reading and writing assignments. I also make clear the time that will be required of each mentee and that the point of the cadence—monthly meetings—is to give them time to do the assignments and practice the assignments within their own organizations. I also make clear that they will only get out of the program what they are willing to put into it. The point is to discover, learn, practice, and form new leadership habits.

Sidenote: I never let a current performance rating be the reason to keep someone from a mentoring circle.

In the case of a low rating, I would have a discussion with the supervisor to understand if their performance was due to their lack of competencies or if their attitude and arrogance were the problem.

On the first call, the prospective mentees are made aware of the level of commitment required for the year, as the course outline is covered along with a discussion of the values that make the year a success for everyone. The five values we cover on the call are (1) attendance, (2) respect, (3) self-development, (4) engagement, and (5) safety (psychological). Without adherence to these, the level of trust needed to bring vulnerability, honesty, humility, and ultimately, change, will not be present. Each of these is unpacked more fully in the workbook.

After the participants have had an opportunity to ask their questions, the mentees are given their first assignments—which include emailing me (or the mentor) their commitment to the mentoring circle and the five values; emailing me (or the mentor) separately with the one area that they feel needs to change in order to become a more effective leader; and choosing a point person to coordinate schedules and locations of the meetings and establish a private, enterprise social media site for posting notes and assignments.

Additionally, I ask them to read *Reading Like a Writer* (Francine Prose, 2006) and have each mentee write their story, APA style, on two pages or fewer. Since all stories follow a narrative disclosing the protagonist, a dilemma or a call to action, a hero, a transformation, and a resolution, I ask the group to watch their favorite sitcom with a pad of paper and pencil to see how each of the five elements unfolds in the half-hour story.

This is a good model for a succinct and well-written story, since the protagonist and dilemma or call to action are generally revealed in the first two minutes of the show. It's easy to write one's story in five or ten pages, but writing it in just two pages is difficult and makes the writer think about what's important to the thread of the story and what makes no difference.

MONTH TWO: SELF-DISCOVERY / SELF-DISCLOSURE

Always remember that you are absolutely unique. Just like everyone else.
—*Margaret Mead*

After an icebreaker and introductions at this first face-to-face meeting, we talk about the assignment and any aha moments they had, especially in watching their TV shows to capture a narrative arc.

As the mentees begin reading their respective stories to the group, it has never failed that there isn't a dry eye in the room when people are done. I try not to hurry the group through this process, leaving space for feedback and questions from the group, creating vulnerability and building trust to set the stage for the transformation ahead that each will encounter.

Perhaps the biggest discovery the group makes is that we are far more similar than we are dissimilar.

MEET JASON

One of the mentees, Jason, was struggling to build trust and kept people at arm's length. His "walls" were challenged early in the process, and it changed everything for him, personally and professionally. He said it this way:

> *My one takeaway from this year starts with the second meeting of the mentoring group. I vividly remember how uncomfortable I was listening to some of my peers tell their emotional stories. There was zero chance that I would open up enough to tell the story of myself, my family, and my son. Now, a short year later, there is zero chance that my story would be about anything else. I see now how my fear of being open about personal things has manifested in many unhealthy ways, both at work and at home. I overused humor to cover for those uncomfortable emotional moments, and now I see how that affected the 'oil in the machine'. I now clearly understand what was causing me to feel like my relationships were good but not great, and that was my fear of letting people in. I didn't trust people*

enough, which was causing me to be an "accidental diminisher."

I open up more and truly learn to trust. I have already started on this journey by telling the story I should have told a year ago. Not only did I send the story of my family's uncertain time to the mentoring team in an email, but to the entire area that I have been entrusted to lead. If I had known years ago how good it feels to share and to get back kind words of support, I could only imagine how much further along personally and professionally I would be today.

Assignments for next month include making story corrections as needed for clarity and reading *Leadership and Self-Deception: Getting Out of the Box* (The Arbinger Institute, 2000). I also encourage them to keep their story fresh and relevant and to keep working on it!

Lastly, without fearing that they would have to read them, I encourage each mentee to write their own obituary. I warn them that it will be difficult and that in the end, it will actually be written by someone else. The point of the exercise is to establish a North Star for one's life and career. This serves as a frame for all of one's decisions, personally and professionally. As Andy Stanley is fond of saying, "What story do you want to tell, when all there is, is a story to tell?"

MONTH THREE: DISCOVERING THE GAPS

An unexamined life is not worth living.
—Socrates

This month's discussion carries over from the previous month's exercise of writing one's story and obituary. Without having mentees read their obituaries, we talk about the difficulty of the exercise and the importance of framing one's present by how one wants to be remembered.

Another mentee named Jason (different from the Jason we met earlier) commented five or six years after our mentoring time on the profound impact of the exercise:

> *The two most important things your mentorship taught me were to think about how I wanted my obituary to read and to manage by behaviors [instead of outcomes], letting the results take care of themselves. I have developed a deep commitment to behavioral management now and understand exactly what you taught me. It has had a profound impact on my career in the last five years. My career advanced dramatically, and as crazy as it sounds, I turned down a promotion to Vice President, because my obituary will read about the*

firm commitment I made to being present for my daughter and being the best dad I can be. Interestingly, I was contacted by several colleagues—including the CEO—with overwhelming support for my decision. I find myself now in a position where I support multiple VPs and play an integral role in setting vision. What you provided is what guides me daily, both professionally and personally.

A follow-on discussion on the reading for the month revealed the group's aha moments regarding the "box" that each is stuck in. What do the attitudes and actions communicate to each of our teams? In the context of getting out of the box, the concept of personal change is introduced to the group.

Then the mentees take a clean sheet of paper and write the three to five words or phrases that come to mind as they think of themselves. We take no more than five minutes for this exercise. Then each folds up the piece of paper and puts it away.

At the heart of this exercise is getting and listening to feedback. Easy to say but hard to do.

Rhett, whom we met earlier, said it this way:

I would say the biggest thing I'm changing [as a result of the mentoring] is asking for feedback. Prior to this journey, I didn't do it often, and I made assumptions about what others thought and what I needed to do or change. I'm actively changing this, and I'm very intentional and diligent about asking for feedback about a wide range of things— small and large. I've also made a conscious effort to ensure that I follow up on that feedback to close the gap and let others know that I value their feedback, I'm listening, and that I'm committed to making some tweaks!

Another of Rhett's colleagues, Gretchen, had this to say about starting with the end in mind:

I have shared this phrase from Dr. Felix dozens of times in the last ten years: "Begin with the end in mind." While it may not have been his personal quote, he spent a great deal of time and effort challenging us to recognize what that looks like for each of us. Furthermore, as he guided us to explore and recognize what tomorrow, next year, or even retirement might look like, it aided in my personal confidence to be the leader of my ship and steer the path I chose, rather than one I could simply follow. Following the completion of his mentoring, I decided to keep writing my story, which led me to take on a new position in another organization across the country. Looking back, I question if I would be where I am today had it not been for [his] discipline, care, and leadership.

Using the discussion and learning from the previous two months, list the areas where they need transformation to increase their leadership effectiveness, and read *Social Intelligence* (Karl Albrecht, 2005).

Have each mentee find ten people to write the first three to four words or phrases that immediately come to mind when thinking of them in their role (make sure to allow for anonymity). After receiving all the assessments, compare the feedback to what they wrote about themselves. Read *Multipliers* (Liz Wiseman and Greg McKeown, 2017, end ed.), and take the test at the back of the book.

MONTH FOUR: MOTIVATOR OR DE-MOTIVATOR?

The joy of leadership comes from seeing others achieve more than they thought they were capable of.
—Simon Sinek

This month's group discussion opens with Liz Wiseman and Greg McKeown's book *Multipliers,* in which they coin the terms *multiplier* and *diminisher* to describe how leaders impact the people in their organizations and, by extension, the performance of their organizations.

I tend to think of this in terms of whether a leader is a motivator for people to stretch and do more than they believed they could, or a de-motivator that unwittingly causes people to work harder just to overcome the leader's dysfunctional style.

As part of the discussion, I led the mentees to identify one or more areas where the energy, problem-solving, and productivity of their respective groups are greater than the sum of the parts and where their behaviors weaken or reduce the total output of the group, however it's measured.

MEET MIKE

Almost every mentee is deeply impacted by Wiseman and McKeown's book, but one of the mentees was particularly impacted by reading *Multipliers*. Mike wrote to me a number of years after our time together with these words:

> *As the book Multipliers taught me, being a "know-it-all" is my diminishing trait. It is the aspect of my leadership that your mentoring has caused me to decide to change the most. I no longer tell people what to do, or even give them the easy answer (if I can help it). I try to let them figure it out safely for themselves [by asking] questions and setting up broader frameworks for them to cultivate their ideas.*

The next part of the discussion is about the results and discoveries from the 360 exercise from the previous month—how we see ourselves versus how others see us. Connecting the dots to personal and professional brands, it generates a productive discussion about our view of self versus others' view of us and, therefore, our leadership effectiveness.

Assignments for next month include writing short-term and long-term goals; defining success; writing a personal/professional brand statement, keeping it to fewer than 140 characters; and reading *Thanks for the Feedback* (Douglas Stone and Sheila Heen, 2014).

MONTH FIVE: WHAT'S YOUR BRAND?

> *The difference between who you are and who you want to be is what you do.*
> **—Unknown**

Using the assignment from the previous month and some well-known brand statements, the group can engage in a discussion of the definition of a brand and how it applies to them. The mentor also facilitates a discussion on *implicit* versus *explicit* brand, with examples of major brand failures because of the misalignment of the two. This will tie directly into their own leadership effectiveness. The opportunity for discovery is that the strength of a brand is measured less by what companies and leaders say or think about *themselves* and more by what *other* people experience.

MEET TOM

One of the mentees we met in the last chapter, Tom, told me that one of the most important lessons he learned from the mentoring experience was the importance of building and owning a strong personal and professional brand. It was a lesson that had guided him for several years since our time together and has helped him frame his decisions about his work, his relationships, and his career.

He said it best this way:

> *I can tell you that being part of the mentoring program that you instituted here at AT&T has been priceless. There have been many things that I have kept close as takeaways from that experience. One . . . that has helped me from our mentoring circle is the building of my own personal brand. I have seen a lot of change throughout the years and in many ways, [but] . . . you taught me to build a brand and to own it. My supervisors and employees have appreciated that, and I thank you for showing me how important brand is, not just to an organization but to the individual as well.*

ROB'S VIEW

One of Tom's colleagues, Rob, contributed to the notion that building and owning one's brand is important in leading people effectively.

> *Based on our time together, the one item that really hit hard for me is clearly being able to "Define my personal brand." I was given a brand by my team as "energetic," an identity I have carried with me every day since. Setting the tone and keeping an upbeat attitude every day for my team has had a big impact on their morale and confidence. I have started helping other managers identify their own "personal brand statement" and begin working towards what they wish to be known for.*

MONTH SIX: REDEFINING SUCCESS

Achievement, like money, doesn't change you—
it only makes you more of who you are!
—Warren Buffett

Success is an important indicator in a society that values hard work and achievement, so with the assignment from the previous month, the mentor facilitates a discussion answering the following questions:

- Are there other dimensions to success besides achievement?
- What are the effects of these on my personal/ professional brand?

We introduce the concept that success is the by-product of great stewardship of resources, not the end goal in itself. This will be a new concept for most people because of our "success equals achievement/ accumulation/accolades" culture.

Referring back to the exercise of writing one's obituary in Month Two, I led a discussion on whether their lives have been defined by achievement, accumulation, and accolades or by relationships and impact.

Here, I recount a story of a division president I knew personally, whose entire life was defined by the traditional elements of success but devoid of any meaningful and impactful relationships. Reading his actual obituary, which his family wrote, was a lesson in having one's success measured by titles and accomplishments rather than relationships.

Jason, whom we met in Month Three, talked about the profound impact this exercise and subsequent discussion had on his personal life, his relationships, and even the trajectory of his career. It should be noted for the reader that the preparation for a discussion of this sort may cause you to rethink your own view of success and the views that you have perhaps unwittingly imposed on others in your organization.

This is a great opportunity—as it was for me—to share your own journey and vulnerabilities in this area.

I want to be careful not to be misunderstood on the issue of redefining success. For organizations and companies, success is ultimately dictated and defined by shareholders. As stewards of any business, we must take care to deliver on those expectations. What I want my mentees to take away from this is that we must not let the responsibilities and rewards of our jobs define who we really are. In the words of Howard Hendricks, we must "not be dissolved by the stream in which we swim."

Assignments for next month include reframing the goals from Month Five; continued work on each mentee's brand statement; preparing questions for a meeting with a more senior executive (at least two levels above the mentees); and a high-level read of *The Extraordinary Leader* (John Zenger and Joseph Folkman, 2002).

MONTH SEVEN:
DISCOVER WHAT IT TAKES

The greatest glory in living lies not in never failing, but in rising every time we fall.
—Nelson Mandela

This session involves getting the mentees to have a peek inside a day-in-the-life (DITL) with a senior executive—someone two or more levels above their level. Using their prepared questions, mentees are able to have a dialogue of exploration to learn about a more senior executive and to gain insight and understanding of the demands of their job.

It almost never failed that when I was visiting employees in the field, someone would have a simplistic solution to all our problems across the division. Of course, it depended on my appointing them to a position of influence, several levels above their current position. But upon further conversation, it became clear that no one had a clue of the demands of that elevated position: the trade-offs, decisions, and demands.

It's easy to have a simplistic or naive view of success at higher leadership levels, but I've found that this session helps junior leaders have a more informed and less critical view of what it takes to lead well at higher levels of the organization. Make sure the executive who comes to speak to the group is humble and vulnerable enough to share their own story, including what they have done well and not so well, how they have risen above setbacks, and what they've learned along the way. An important part of this is a discussion about the behaviors, habits, competencies, and perspectives required to be effective at leading at that level.

Any executive who has nothing to share about what they would have done over, or differently, likely isn't going to inspire the mentees. As I've told every group of mentees I've ever led, "There's nothing more dangerous than a leader who can't admit they were wrong."

This is also the session to "open the veil" as it were, and have an honest discussion of how junior and upwardly mobile executives are evaluated—formally and informally—by the senior executive ranks of the company. There is nothing more discouraging and disheartening to aspiring leaders than to miss the unspoken rules of the road within an organization and languish in the middle management ranks, feeling stuck. Anything that is important to understand about the company, its market, its competitors, and its important metrics as viewed by investors is worth discussing in this session.

Assignments for next month include revising their brand statement, as necessary; evaluating their transformation plan for validity and effectiveness; assessing the "cost" to achieve their stated transformation; performing an audit of their weekly time checkbook (daily writing down the number of hours spent on major activities); setting up one-on-one time for feedback from the mentor, as desired; and reading *Our Iceberg Is Melting* (John Kotter and Holger Rathgeber, 2005).

MONTH EIGHT:
REFRAME YOUR LEADERSHIP

You have brains in your head. You have feet in your shoes. You can steer yourself any direction you choose.
—Dr. Suess

This month's discussion uses a Leadership Force Analysis, often used in campaigns, product launches, and debate preparation, enabling the mentees to see which forces support their intended transformation and which forces resist it. These can also be thought of as strengths and unintended consequences or as past behaviors and habits versus future behaviors and habits.

Using the time checkbook audit from the previous month and the Asset Accounts framework—Competencies, Currencies, Quality of Life, and Significance—discuss how each of these "asset accounts" relates to each other. The point to be made is that making the right "deposits" into the right accounts at the right time will determine if and how to get to the most important asset account—Significance.

The unspoken cry of the human heart is, *Do I matter?*

People spend a career and a lifetime accumulating without ever answering that question. Since everyone has the same asset accounts, how much of our 168 hours each week are spent investing in which accounts, and in which order?

Mike K. said the following:

> *It is hard to name a single thing that had the most impact on me over the past year's mentoring. Some of the exercises, the revelations that they brought, and then getting to share them with my teams was impactful. Doing the 168 was especially eye-opening. The reading list really helped expand my thinking around leadership. Since my time with Mike, my career has led me through several roles in leadership and influence, including: Area Manager, Designer, Project Manager, Project Manager II, Senior Project Manager, and Director across three companies. This is a success that I couldn't have envisioned for myself when I began with those mentoring sessions. It has also paid dividends in my personal life, helping me to build and strengthen relationships with family, friends, and neighbors. This, in turn, has led to additional collaborations with other industries that would otherwise not have been available to me. For example, I was able to develop a friendship with the COO of a dark-fiber company that ended up being an important client of ours.*

Kerry said, "Mike accomplished this through a skilled balance of direction and guided reflection. A specific exercise, called the 'Checkbook of Time,' was very meaningful to the group."

Assignments for next month include identifying one area in their business that needs to change and come with a realistic plan to change it; identifying the metric or outcome that will signal success for the transformation; and reading *Influencer: The Power to Change Anything* (K. Patterson, J. Grenny, D. Maxfield, E. Conger, and A. Switzler, 2007).

MONTH NINE: CHANGE

If you don't like change, you're going to like irrelevance even less.
—General (Ret.) Eric Shinseki

We start with a discussion about organizational change and its many dimensions, including decision time, execution time, productivity, and outcomes, to name a few. Using *Our Iceberg is Melting,* we discuss the eight steps to organizational change, which the mentor can use to facilitate the discussion.

Using *Influencer,* the mentor facilitates the discovery process for the two essential questions everyone answers and the three levels of behavioral change—in oneself and in organizations. This is an important discussion, especially in large organizations where heavy investments in training, education, information, rewards and recognition, compensation, and even discipline are thought to be the best moderators of behavior change.

The month's discussion ends with learning the art of the question—insightful and leading questions—as a way to help people open up within their own assumptions, challenge their own thinking, and embrace the necessary change for better outcomes.

Rob, whom we met earlier, discovered the ripple effect that occurs when a leader decides to embrace change.

> One thing that I have decided to change in my Leadership revolves around my personal brand statement, "Practice Optimism." I discovered it isn't always about being just a cheerleader and giving encouraging pep talks to my team. It's moving to have more optimism and to set an example for my team. This has been contagious, and it has started to inspire others around me. Since I began focusing on being more optimistic, improving my body language, and enhancing my communication, I've noticed a significant improvement in collaboration and engagement within my team this year. The team and I have been quicker to move on to new endeavors and are willing to try new

opportunities within our entire [operating area].

The assignment for next month: reading *The Speed of Trust* (Stephen M. R. Covey, 2005).

MONTH TEN: BUILDING TRUST AND ENGAGEMENT

> *Leaders establish trust with candor, transparency, and credit.*
> —Jack Welch

Using *Speed of Trust* as a reference, the mentor can lead a discussion on ways to build trust in the organization or on the team. Referencing *Social Intelligence* and the mentees' rewritten brand statements as facilitation tools, the mentor can lead a discussion on ways they might be more empathetic in their relationships, more authentic with their leadership, and better at picking up on nonverbal cues as one of their feedback channels.

With these two building blocks in place, this month's session concludes with a discussion on building engagement with their respective teams. As the best moderator of outcomes and the highest predictor of organizational performance, engagement is often misunderstood or mistaken for job satisfaction or involvement. There are four key dimensions to engagement, according to the research, and six key cultural elements that must be in place to ensure employee engagement.

Brian—one of the leadership trainers in a support organization—commented on the effect that the mentoring circles had on the organization:

> *Your organization is the singular example I use when I talk to other organizations about successful change management and engagement. I truly appreciate the opportunity to have learned from your example.*

Assignments for the next month include scheduling one-on-one time with the mentor, if desired, for end-of-year feedback; starting a journal (if it hasn't already been started) of key learnings from the mentoring circle; finding and documenting the five to eight behavioral predictors of success for their direct-reports; and reading *Difficult Conversations* (Douglas Stone, Bruce Patton, and Sheila Heen, 2000).

MONTH ELEVEN: LEADERSHIP LESSONS

> *Don't judge each day by the harvest you reap,*
> *but by the seeds that you plant.*
> **—Robert Louis Stevenson**

Starting with a discussion of the principles learned in *Difficult Conversations*, this month's discussion is the mentor's opportunity to talk about principles that have been an integral part of his or her success. These include having timely, informal, and honest feedback for people; the ongoing importance of mentors and role models; choosing friends wisely; the commitment to investing in self and developing others as good stewardship; finding the strengths that make a difference and elevating them; and the necessity and process for hiring good people.

Gretchen, whom we met earlier and was one of my early-on mentees, commented on this point:

> *Dr. Felix's formal mentoring group allowed me the opportunity to surround myself with other leaders from other states to learn perspective, best practices, and generate innovative ideas. I completed his mentorship with a deeper sense of knowledge as to who I was and, more importantly, who I wanted to be.*

The process and structure for making good hiring decisions are discussed in greater detail in the workbook and are based on both research and empirical evidence. It can be a useful tool in organizations where psychological and personality assessments are not available in the hiring process—generally true of most organizations except at very senior levels. Most people tend to hire based on liking someone, albeit subconsciously, instead of hiring by behavioral predictors of success.

Assignment for Month Twelve is to read *The Power of the Other* (Henry Cloud, 2016).

MONTH TWELVE: COMMITTING TO THE JOURNEY

> *Find a great mentor who believes in you; your life will change forever!*
> —Bill Walsh

The last meeting is a celebration. I always host a dinner in my home, giving everyone permission to travel as necessary to participate. Over hors d'oeuvres, drinks, and dinner, we spend time talking about the most impactful lessons learned from the year and the importance of making personal and professional growth a journey and not a destination.

Tom captured the essence of paying it forward perfectly:

> *Through all the changes that I experienced over the past twenty-five-plus years, you are the only leader of the business who took time to invest in me personally. I do all that I can to follow your lead and work to invest in my team at every opportunity."* Gretchen echoed the sentiment: "I'm forever grateful for that formal mentorship opportunity and have passed on his learnings to countless others

in my career. It has been a privilege to learn
from you.

This conversation includes things such as ways people can stay connected, the importance of finding mentors, ways to keep their respective stories fresh, and having recovery mechanisms for when they fall short in any area of their development.

To reinforce the reading for this month, I leave the group with a recitation of the history lesson posted on the wall of the Maritime Museum in Astoria, Oregon, at the mouth of the Columbia River. The story elucidates how experienced bar pilots are used to navigating ships of all sizes around and through the shifting sandbars where the mighty Columbia River meets the ocean currents of the Pacific Ocean to safe passage inside the mouth of the Columbia. The story is a powerful metaphor for the importance of having people around us who are experienced and can help us keep from running afoul of the sandbars in our careers.

HEARING FROM THE MENTEES

Almost all the people who write to me about their experience in a mentoring group end their note by commenting on the impact it had on their life and career.

> *The way you made yourself available and*
> *approachable was truly inspiring to many*
> *of us, not just me.*

You have had and will continue to have a very positive impact on me, and again, I just wanted to say thank you.

Thank you again for everything that you have done for me over the last year.

You have played a very important role in helping me be a better leader, and I'm very grateful for this .... I would like to thank you from the bottom of my heart for your time, valuable insights, and commitment to me.

I would also like to thank you for the candid discussions, your time, and providing the platform for me to bond with my peer group. The sharing of knowledge and the support have truly been a blessing.

Thanks again for this mentoring session, without a doubt, and no matter what the future holds, it has changed my life for the better.

Thank you for your time, input, and wisdom!

[You] created a culture that encouraged the team to WANT to contribute and be part of

something bigger than themselves. That is a legacy we all should strive to achieve.

Thank you for noticing my aspirations and giving me an opportunity to learn from you. I look forward to continuing to learn from you and to applying the lessons you've shared as I move forward in my career.

Thank you for investing your time in me. I greatly appreciate the time and resources you have provided. It has been life-changing!

The lessons learned will stick with me for life. You took the time to invest in me, and I will continue to pay it forward.

Our year together was extremely impactful to me, and I very sincerely thank you for it. You are an inspiring and amazing Multiplier!

What you provided is what guides me daily, both professionally and personally.

By the end of our time together, the mentees return to their respective organizations to practice all that they learned with the knowledge and assurance that they have a champion and cheerleader in me. Most importantly, they know that if they fail or get discouraged, they have each other to talk to and are always welcome to reach out to me. No great leader ever gets to the top by themselves. In the immortal words of author Alex Haley, "If you see a turtle on a fencepost, you know he had some help."

7

A CHARGE TO MENTORS AND EXECUTIVE SPONSORS

> *Don't judge each day by the harvest you reap,*
> *but by the seeds that you plant.*
> —**Robert Louis Stevenson**

Unless you're an executive in a government agency specifically dedicated to promoting equity and inclusion, your current position is likely due to your ability to deliver consistent results and improve them year after year. If you've been in business for any length of time and have tackled quality issues, you understand that achieving better outcomes begins with examining your inputs. Always start by addressing the root causes.

Attempting to *fix* results by *forcing* results is a fool's game. The same is true for getting a diverse organization all the way to the C-suite. If your goal is to build a truly diverse organization, you must start by ensuring qualified diverse candidates are present at your entry points and by maintaining diverse representation in a structured development program.

The term *facilitated* is purposeful in that you can't leave it to employees to self-assess and figure out their own development needs.

A former client of mine was perplexed at their lack of ability to find diverse candidates for entry-level positions in their highly specialized professional services company. They had lost sight of the importance of making small investments of time and resources in local trade schools and college prep programs to spark interest in the types of jobs they offered. Getting more kids interested in their jobs before they get into higher education would be a great way to start broadening the diversity of applicants.

This is a great example of solving for first causes. Lest you worry that the cost of this type of program will be a drain on your earnings, let me reassure you that this type of program has a positive return on investment. Without even comparing what you currently spend on DEI-related initiatives, programs, and employees (in the federal government, that number is staggering—measured in tens of billions of dollars) to the increase in returns from a well-run mentoring program, you can easily justify a program of this type from the increase in employee engagement and the resulting increase in performance.

The biggest problem the nation has—relative to employment—isn't unemployment. It is employee engagement. The US government spends around $60 to $80 billion per year on unemployment benefits. Studies show that fully engaged employees are twice as productive as employees who are only partially engaged or disengaged.

Moving the GDP just 1 percent by increasing employee engagement would bring in an extra $400 billion. Before you push back with a claim that all your employees are fully engaged, let me share that both Pew Research and Gallup have shown for more than a decade that two-thirds of US employees report that they are not engaged or only partially engaged in their jobs. That means that the average company has only about one-third of its employees who are fully engaged and therefore providing two-thirds of their productivity.

You might say that your company is better than average with engagement, but even if you're twice as good as the average, you still have a third of your employees who are a drag on your productivity. If you could improve your productivity equation by just 5 percent by increasing employee engagement, you will have more than paid for your efforts to invest in your employees through mentoring.

I know firsthand because it happened in my own organization. Even employees who were not in the program at the time became more engaged because they were either practicing what they learned while in the program, or they wanted to be noticed by their bosses to be selected for the next class in the program.

In less than three years, the organization I was leading went from last place among five peer organizations to first place. If you think that was a trivial move, consider that the over $25 million increase in financial returns driven by better engagement and less attrition (from 28 percent to 11 percent) was more than twenty times the costs associated with the mentoring program. But even if your efforts returned a quarter of my results, you'd have five times the return for the costs of your mentoring program.

Engagement, however, has several dimensions to it. I won't go into all of them here—that's a subject for a different book. There is one dimension, nevertheless, that is important to mentoring worth unpacking here—psychological safety.

The mentor must be sensitive to the emotional and psychological needs of the mentees, if he/ she truly wants to have an impact. This is the essence of building a relationship that matters. It can be seen in the "chemistry" between mentor and mentee—a chemistry that inspires greatness.

In the passages of the ancient scriptures, there is a story of Elijah—a prophet for the Israelites— and Elisha, his understudy. Elijah so inspired Elisha that when it was time for Elijah to end his ministry, he granted Elisha anything he wanted. Elisha, for his part, wanted only one thing: a double portion of Elijah's spirit.

What's the point here? It is the mentor's duty to build the chemistry that overcomes the mentee's reticence and that builds confidence and inspiration.

I offer a warning to you as a sponsor for this type of program. Don't try to keep the culture of DEI and lay a program of this sort over it to mask or legitimize your decision-making efforts for hiring and promotions. This works against the kind of inspiration we just mentioned because at its core. DEI discriminates in order to check the right boxes. If you try to keep the old culture, you'll keep the same results. Without changing the culture, you won't address the root causes of your diversity challenges. As a result, you'll make hiring and promotion decisions through a misguided lens, while subtly trying to control the outcomes.

To make a lasting impact on performance, hiring and promotion decisions should be based solely on competence, merit, and performance predictors (behaviors). Any other lens for hiring or promoting is only going to have an adverse effect on your organization and its brand when a crisis arises, and you need the highest level of competence to respond and lead. If you intend to engage in a program of this sort, you might assign it to someone to administer, but the one thing you cannot delegate is the face of commitment to the program.

You must be as engaged in the development and administration of this program as you expect both the mentors and the mentees to be. This happens by ensuring the right mentors are installed. Not every senior executive will make a great mentor. Take the time to identify which of your executives truly excel in this role—those who have a genuine passion for people, are dedicated to your diversity initiatives, and are equally committed to driving results for your stakeholders.

Your engagement is further reflected in the time you commit and allow others to dedicate to the program. This is evident in the effort you invest in establishing, promoting, and regularly reviewing the program, and you may choose to be periodically involved in the program.

I was always impressed that Jack Welch, a renowned American business executive and author, best known for his tenure as the CEO of General Electric (GE), regularly attended and spoke at the GE leadership training programs.

At a minimum, your time as a sponsor is well-spent meeting with mentors and occasionally visiting mentoring circles. However, if you choose to get involved, just remember that you can only expect what you're willing to inspect.

Another aspect of your time commitment as a program sponsor is ensuring that everyone has a fair opportunity to participate and receive mentorship. It is important to see the mentee landscape as an opportunity to invest in people who have potential but might not otherwise get a chance to develop into a productive leaders.

That's not to say that you should exclude some in order to allow others to participate. My only point is to be purposefully inclusive with your selection of those who get mentored.

The final element of your time commitment to this program is paying attention to the material used in the curriculum. I have compiled the literature I've used over the years, which has positively impacted individuals and mentoring circles. These books have influenced discussions, led to behavior changes, and ultimately improved performance and career outcomes.

My recommendation is that if you modify the material, ensure that you don't alter the core intent of the program. Stay focused on self-discovery and openness, committing to personal and professional growth, identifying effective feedback mechanisms, developing an authentic style that fosters trust and engagement, and enhancing organizational performance.

For your convenience, if you elect to use the material I have outlined, there is an associated workbook that is available upon request and will soon be available in published form. You can reach out to me via LinkedIn (Mike Felix, Ph.D.) or my website (mikefelixphd.com) or through email (mike@mikefelixphd.com). I am also available to speak to your leadership organization and to "train the trainer" for sponsors and/or mentors.

8

A CHARGE TO MENTEES

Find a great mentor who believes in you; your
life will change forever!
—Bill Walsh

If you've picked up this book because you're hoping for someone to invest in you, helping you level the playing field for key assignments or promotions, I have good news. It's possible to create that kind of environment in your company or organization, and you have the potential to be the influencer who makes it happen.

This book would not have been possible without the bravery of Janet, whom you met in chapter 1. She asked me to help her develop the skills and competencies she needed to interview on equal footing with others. Being brave enough to ask a senior executive for mentoring or a program where you and others can be mentored will tell you everything you need to know about whether executive management is truly interested in developing people.

You might be surprised to know that there is receptivity to your request; it's just that no one ever asked them before.

You're likely reading this book because you realize that you can't get there by yourself. Like the turtle on the fencepost on Alex Haley's desk, any honest senior executive would acknowledge that the same applies to them: they had some help. They arrived where they were because someone invested in them.

A valuable life skill that will also benefit your professional life is learning to ask for what you want. It's often said that people never get 100 percent of what they don't ask for. The very same is true for getting mentored. These days, in addition to leading occasional mentoring circles, I spend time in one-on-one mentoring and coaching for young and emerging leaders who have asked me or one of my close friends for someone who could coach them to be a more effective leader.

Sometimes it helps if you find like-minded colleagues who desire the same thing. Knowing that there is a ready-made mentoring circle is often just the impetus needed for a senior executive to step up and sponsor a program. Be thoughtful in your approach, and never make your potential sponsor or mentor feel threatened if you don't get the desired outcome. If it helps, you can elect to use the material I have outlined in an associated workbook, which is available upon request.

Aside from finding a group of colleagues and presenting the material, there are two pieces of advice I have for you. The first is to commit to doing the hard work of introspection, self-disclosure, change, and building the skills of a highly effective leader. This is not an easy thing to do, but if you do it well, you will likely rise to levels that less committed people will not get. In merit-based organizations, those who work the hardest are rewarded with greater opportunity.

I can tell you from experience that there is nothing more inspiring to a mentor than to find people who are serious about being the best version of themselves that they can be. In the mentoring circles I have led over the past decade or so, there have only been two people that I can remember who have not committed to this work.

How do I know? They would attend the monthly meetings without completing their assignments, which led to a lack of significant or meaningful contributions to the discussions. Given the time I invest in preparing to lead these discussions, it's always discouraging. I view it as a sign of disrespect for my time and the effort their colleagues put into the process.

The second and last piece of advice I have for you is to be as humble as you can be. Real humility, not the false one, which is often disguised as insecurity or self-deprecating humor in search of a compliment. These group discussions are not a competition to see who has the most extreme experience—good or bad— as if to communicate "I can top that" to your colleagues and the mentor. Humility is demonstrated in your willingness to let someone with more experience "pilot the ship."

Pay attention to the story of the Maritime Museum inside the mouth of the Columbia River in chapter 6. Any ship's captain too proud to ask for help from an experienced pilot will likely run his ship aground. There are more than two thousand ships buried in the sandbars, caused by captains who were too proud to admit that there was someone better than themselves to navigate the winds, seas, and shifting sandbars. To not recognize this is to put your own career in great peril. To this day, the US Coast Guard averages sixty rescues per month of ships and vessels that attempt to navigate the turbulent waters at the mouth of the Columbia without the right experience.

My prayer is that if you desire to lead well, you'll go after the things that matter most to your effectiveness. They are within your reach!

ACKNOWLEDGMENTS

This book has been several years in the making, and for anyone who has dared to write, you know it takes many people to be part of the process: colleagues, mentors, encouragers, friends, and family.

In that vein, I'd like to thank the team at StoryBuilders—especially Jen and Jesse—without whom this project would have never seen the light of day.

To those who were part of one of the many mentoring circles I led over the years, thank you for teaching me how to be a better mentor. You'll never know how much I learned from you. You were the inspiration for this book.

To my senior team, when these mentoring circles were being started, thank you for helping select mentees who would have otherwise been overlooked.

Thank you to the authors and thought leaders who made personal investments in me along the way. You inspired and encouraged me. Liz Wiseman, Sheila Heen, Doug Stone, and Karl Clauson, I have learned something invaluable from each of you, and you have given freely of your time and expertise.

To Dr. Billy Browning, for your investment in me and the more than forty years of friendship, mentoring, conversations, and challenging me to be the best version of myself, thank you seems wholly inadequate. Warren Buffett was right about choosing friends wisely because they influence the path our lives take. Your quiet influence in my career and leadership is manifested in the pages of this book.

To my kids, Joshua, Sarah Beth, and Hannah; my son-in-law, Rey, and daughter-in-law, Stephanie; along with my four grandkids, Giada, Noelle, Emma, and Sam—each of you have been a great source of encouragement for me, as you have kept me grounded in what's important and have taught me the importance of authenticity in relationships. You have all inspired me to see this through to completion. Thank you.

My mom and dad, Carol and Mickey, along with my late mother-in-law, Dorothy Stanton, were the original inspiration in my pursuit of the career I enjoyed for more than forty-three years. Each consistently showed interest in my career, development, and work through the years. Thank you for being constant sources of encouragement to get this book written.

Lastly, and most importantly, to my wife, Bethany, thank you for the years of support and encouragement. You have been there every step of the way, graciously hosting mentoring circles in our home and making each one of them feel like they were part of our family, encouraging me to turn the years of experience and investment in others into something that might inspire other executives. Thank you for supporting me through the times when I wanted to give up and abandon this project. Your love, encouragement, and support made all this possible.

ABOUT THE AUTHOR

Dr. Mike Felix is a seasoned executive, leadership mentor, and trusted adviser with more than forty-three years of experience in the telecom and technology industries. Over the course of his career, he has held senior executive and C-suite roles, leading key divisions at a Fortune 50 company and spearheading several successful venture-capital-backed start-ups and turnarounds.

Passionate about leadership development, Dr. Felix has dedicated much of his career to mentoring the next generation of executives. As an executive sponsor for leadership training initiatives, he has personally coached and mentored more than on hundred junior executives and emerging leaders, helping them cultivate authentic and effective leadership styles.

In 2018, he founded Legacy Point Advisors to continue this mission, providing mentorship and strategic guidance to leaders and organizations in the areas of culture, change management, strategy, hiring practices, and employee engagement.

Beyond his corporate contributions, Dr. Felix has served on the boards of more than fifteen organizations—spanning technology companies, venture capital firms, investment banks, public policy forums, university foundations, and high-impact nonprofits and ministries.

Dr. Felix holds a B.S. in Electrical Engineering, an M.A. in Psychology, and a Ph.D. in Media Psychology. Today, he remains deeply committed to shaping the future of leadership through mentorship, advisory roles, and thought leadership.

Connect with Mike at mikefelixphd.com; on LinkedIn at Mike Felix, Ph.D.; or through email at mike@mikefelixphd.com.

ENDNOTES

[1] In 1969, Laurence Peter observed a management behavior whereby people in a hierarchy tend to rise to a level of incompetence.

[2] Richard E. Nisbett and Timothy DeCamp Wilson, "Telling More Than We Can Know; Verbal Reports on Mental Processes," *Psychological Review* (May 1977).

[3] Lillian T. Eby, Tammy D. Allen, Susan C. Evans, Timothy W. Ng, and David L. DuBois, "Does Mentoring Matter? A Multidisciplinary Meta-Analysis of the Mentoring Literature," *Journal of Vocational Behavior* 72, no. 2 (2008): 254–267, https://doi.org/10.1016/j.jvb.2007.04.005.

[4] David Livermore, *Driven by Difference* (AMACOM, 2016).

[5] "Women and Men in STEM Often at Odds Over Workplace Equity," Pew Research Center, Jan. 9, 2018.

[6] J. L. Lee, P. Dave, Reuters News Service, November 1, 2018.

[7] "Stand Up: Set Your Own Course at SNHU," SNHU commercial, December 2017 to December 2021.

[8] David A. Thomas and John J. Gabarro, *Breaking Through: The Making of Minority Executives in Corporate America* (Harvard Business School Press, 1999).

[9] David A. Thomas and John J. Gabarro, *Breaking Through: The Making of Minority Executives in Corporate America* (Harvard Business School Press, 1999).

[10] "Mentoring: A Key to Developing Female Talent," Catalyst (2011), https://www.catalyst.org/research/mentoring-a-key-to-developing-female-talent/.

[11] Jim Collins, Good to Great: *Why Some Companies Make the Leap . . . and Others Don't* (HarperBusiness, 2001).

[12] Jack W. Zenger and Joseph R. Folkman, *The Extraordinary Leader: Turning Good Managers into Great Leaders* (McGraw-Hill, 2002).

[13] Bill Hybels, *Courageous Leadership: Staying Strong in the Face of Adversity* (Zondervan, 2002).

14 Richard E. Nisbett and Timothy DeCamp Wilson, "Telling More Than We Can Know: Verbal Reports on Mental Processes," *Psychological Review* 84, no. 3 (1977): 231–259, https://doi.org/10.1037/0033-295X.84.3.231.

15 Edwin Catmull and Amy Wallace, *Creativity, Inc.: Overcoming the Unseen Forces That Stand in the Way of True Inspiration* (Transworld Publishers Limited, 2014).

16 Abraham H. Maslow, *The Psychology of Science: A Reconnaissance* (Scientific Psychology 1966).

17 Dee Hock, *Birth of the Chaordic Age* (Berrett-Koehler Publishers, 1999).

18 James M. Kouzes and Barry Z. Posner, *The Leadership Challenge: How to Make Extraordinary Things Happen in Organizations*, 6th ed. (Wiley, 2017).

19 Patrick Lencioni, *The Three Signs of a Miserable Job: A Fable for Managers (And Their Employees)* (Jossey-Bass, 2007).

20 Kim S Cameron, "Transformational Leadership and Organizational Culture," *Public Administration Quarterly* (1997).

21 Kim S. Cameron and Sergiusz Moscovici, "Organizational Culture and Change: A Critical Review, *Journal of Applied Behavioral Science* 24, no. 3 (1988): 281–298.

22 Marshall McLuhan, *The Medium Is the Message: An Inventory of Effects* (Bantam Books, 1967).

23 Simon Sinek, *Start with Why: How Great Leaders Inspire Everyone to Take Action* (Penguin Group, 2009).

24 Bill Hybels, *Courageous Leadership: Staying Strong in the Face of Adversity* (Zondervan, 2002).